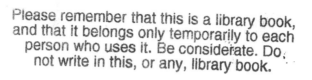

Children of
Alcoholism

Children of Alcoholism

A SURVIVOR'S MANUAL

---

by

Judith S. Seixas and Geraldine Youcha

Crown Publishers, Inc. New York

Excerpt which appears on page 131 is from *Growing Up* by Russel Baker. Reprinted with the permission of Congdon & Weed, Inc., 298 Fifth Avenue, New York, New York.

Material which appears on page 185 is from *What Is Psychotherapy?* by Sidney Bloch, published in 1982. Reprinted with the permission of Oxford University Press, Walton Street, Oxford OX2 6DP, England.

Material which appears on page 68 is from *Children of Alcoholics: a 20-Year Longitudinal Study* by Dorothy Miller and Michael Jang. Copyright © 1977, National Association of Social Workers, Inc. Reprinted with permission from *Social Work Research and Abstracts*, Vol. 13, No. 4 (Winter 1977), page 23, Table 4.

Questions which appear on page 108 from the C.A.S.T. test are reprinted by permission of the author, J. W. Jones, *Children of Alcoholics Screening Test* (C.A.S.T.), Chicago: Camelot Press, 1983. The C.A.S.T. can be ordered from Camelot Press, Attention: Dr. John Johns, 1812 Rolling Green Curve, Mendota Heights, Minnesota 55118.

Published by Crown Publishers, Inc., 225 Park Avenue South, New York, New York 10003
Printed in the United States of America

Library of Congress Cataloging-in-Publication Data

Seixas, Judith S.
Children of alcoholism.

Bibliography: p.
1. Children of alcoholic parents—United States—
Case studies. 2. Alcoholics—United States—Family
relationships—Case studies.   I. Youcha, Geraldine.
II. Title.
HV5132.S44   1985   362.8'2   84-17450
ISBN 0-517-55599-9

10 9 8 7 6

This book is for our parents
and our children

Contents

Acknowledgments

In order to write this book I gathered stories, thoughts, passions, and reminiscences from those who live or have lived with family alcoholism. To them I owe enormous gratitude. Without them I could not have begun.

To the "Saturday morning group" I owe a special debt. They must remain nameless, but without them and Marjorie Levitan this book would be a great deal less than it is.

There are others whose encouragement helped me understand that I had something to say and helped me say it. First, my husband, Frank, whose technical knowledge of alcoholism was a constant resource. Then my children, Peter, Abby, and Noah, whose faith in me was there from the start. And my sister, Brenda Engel, whose clarity of thought and knowledge of the English language pulled me out of sticky places. My cousin Susan Hirschman, editor-in-chief of Greenwillow Books, told me I could do it. Then Anne Martin helped me begin, Ellen Morehouse, with her positive enthusiasm, kept me working, Celia Dulfano never let me forget family dynamics, and Carol Hulsizer contributed some much-needed "last aid." To all, my heartfelt thanks.

Judith S. Seixas

Special thanks are due to Miriam Poser, whose expert knowledge and guidance helped shape this book, and to Joan King, whose enthusiasm and experience are woven into its fabric. My husband, Zeke, contributed unfailing support and the benefit of his professional advice. And my children, Vicky, Sharon, and Joe, were, as usual, patient and encouraging.

                                                    Geraldine Youcha

And we both thank Dan Lewis of the National Council on Alcoholism, whose help has been invaluable.

Introduction

There are at least 22 million adults in this country who have lived with an alcoholic parent. Most have survived the ordeal and are now out on their own. Nearly all of them, however, live with scars, psychic or physical, as a consequence of parental alcoholism. The quality of their lives ranges from devastation and misery to relative fulfillment and happiness.

Most of the survivors view themselves as having been through a unique experience; no other household could have been like their own. Because of the nature of alcoholism itself, they have been unable to talk about what went on in their families. Nor have they been able to talk about the loneliness and terror they felt as they grew up. When asked what it was like, most will simply say their parents were "bananas" or use some glib phrase and go on from there to relate a horror story.

If you struggled to grow up in a home where at least one parent drank too much, you probably have strong feelings, convictions, and biases that are rooted in how your family appeared to you. When behavior fluctuates, or is bizarre, extreme, or inappropriate, the young person is baffled and will often come to conclusions that spring from partial understanding or from understanding distorted by emotional reactions.

Certainly there is a recognizable thread that runs through the fabric of family life in households in which someone is drinking too much. It is the specific characteristics of that thread that will be identified in this book so you will see that you, as the child of at least one alcoholic, are one of many and that your problems can be confronted and viewed in the light of what went on as you and others like you grew up.

Alcoholism is a mysterious illness—an illness that defies logic. Why do some people, who most of the time appear to be in their right minds, continue to drink when they know perfectly well that they are harming their families, their friends, and their own bodies? And why do some people continue to drink when they know the consequences of what they are doing and what will happen if they continue? One explanation is that they are *not* in their "right minds." As the alcoholic continues to drink, the drug acts on the brain to create mental changes; so it is irrational for us to expect rational behavior in someone who continues to drink large amounts of alcohol over a long period of time.

It is incredibly difficult for people who are not themselves in the grip of a substance to understand the power of addiction and how that power takes over. In some ways it can be likened to the insistence of a habit such as fingernail biting or smoking. These are compulsive behaviors most people would undoubtedly like to give up. They hate them. They know how unattractive others find them and how self-destructive they are. And yet most find they can't give them up.

Why does alcoholism continue to be such a monumental problem in our culture? There are many reasons. Most of us are swamped daily, through the media, with powerful messages. They tell us that drinking will make us rich, beautiful, sexy, free, or successful or will carry us (don't ask how) to a beach in a warm, exotic land. These continuous entreaties to drink keep us from developing rational attitudes based on our own experience. We then combine the facts we have learned with the myths we want to believe.

Alcoholism continues to be rampant in our country because alcohol is a drug that "works" for most people. It makes them feel good; it remains an available, relatively cheap social lubricant. It has been called "the solution for every problem." It is a great drug, but it is great only for those who can use it in moderation; for those who can stay out from under its spell; and for those who will act responsibly so that drinking doesn't become "a problem for every solution." For the one out of ten who cannot control the intake of alcohol, it is a dangerous pleasure. It is dangerous too, for those who live and grow up with someone who drinks too much.

The residues of childhood are with you through life. Shakespeare put it well in *The Tempest:* "What is past is prologue." Your childhood will not go away. As you look back, understanding the origins of your problem may help to reduce their impact. Even now you may not be totally aware of the strength of that impact and how often it gets in your way.

These distortions can be corrected so you can more fully understand what happened, why it happened, and the degree to which you are still affected. Perhaps you will be able to use this new understanding to live a life with less guilt, less confusion, less ambivalence, fewer fears, and more of the clear feelings of self-confidence that any adult needs in order to mature.

The case histories in this book are real. They come from the more than 200 children of alcoholics we have talked with as friends, in passing conversations, or in treatment. Details have been changed to protect their privacy. These people have voluntarily shared the experiences of their childhoods. They have taught us what it is like to live in a family askew because of alcoholism. We are grateful to them for giving us a glimpse of their pains, concerns, fears, and shames. When they shared more than a snatch of their lives they presented their feelings so vividly that we could not but sense the enormity of their struggle.

Neither of us is the child of an alcoholic parent, so we can only relay and interpret what has been said to us. At times, this has seemed to be a disadvantage because, as one friend said, "You haven't been there. You can't know." But we have been there— our "there" is a different place, but one that also has its hurts, fears, and sadness. The child of an alcoholic goes through unique experiences related to the nature of alcoholism. However, the disastrous effects upon the individual may not differ so much from the consequences of other difficult situations that most of us are subjected to as we grow up.

It could happen that, if you are the child of an alcoholic, you will find familiar scenes here. Their emotional impact may startle you as you read. Presumably you were not unscathed by what you lived through and still may feel some of the anger, fear, and sadness of your childhood. When you recognize that you are not alone and that the burden of your childhood can be lightened, you may feel relieved.

PART I

Living in Chaos

1

The Terrible Family Secret

> I always had one best friend and even though we talked about what seemed like everything, we never shared the big secret. My secret was my father's drinking; hers was her uncle's. Only recently have we discovered that we both had been sexually molested: me by my father, she by her uncle.
>
> Elaine, Age 30

Come into the house where alcoholism lives. Open the front door. There's the living room. Everything is in perfect order. It looks ready for a photographer or, perhaps, a funeral. On the far side a door swings open for a glimpse into the kitchen. This, the heart of the house, reeks of dirty dishes left in the sink, food-encrusted plates on the table, overflowing garbage. An invisible barrier divides the kitchen from the living room. Just as you—a guest—won't be allowed on the kitchen side, the children of the house aren't allowed on the other side. The public façade is maintained in the living room, while the private chaos is hidden from view. But the disorder of alcoholism cannot be totally hidden, for a closer look reveals another level of reality: The plumped-up pillow on the pink couch doesn't quite cover an empty whiskey bottle.

What is going on? Why the disparity between front and back? Why the attempted cover-up? This orderly-disorderly house is the outward evidence of an extensive denial system that began with the alcoholic (who is both the subject and the main keeper of the secret) and that by now has implicated the whole family.

The pretense that everything is all right in the "for visitors

3

only" living room reflects the pretense that everything is all right in the family. Outsiders must see only what has been arranged for them to see; the chaos has to be hidden; the boat must not be rocked and everything must look fine.

The children who live here are almost, but not quite, misled into thinking that their household is like any other. They want to believe in this normality. One woman said she thought it "unusual" that her mother put vodka in her morning coffee, but her mother reassured her by saying, "This is the way to get the day going right." Not until these children venture beyond their mothers' skirts (or jeans) does it dawn on them that something is definitely different about their own family; and it is then that they begin to wonder what is normal, and if they themselves are crazy. They live a game of "let's pretend, let's protect," yet guarding the secret protects neither the alcoholic nor the children.

They quickly learn to conceal what happens at home from outsiders as well as from close relatives, concluding that if even a grandparent—perhaps the drinker's father or mother—shouldn't know, there must be something immoral, sinful, or criminal about the drinking. These children see alcoholism not as an illness but as a weakness, an embarrassment—and as a shame that accumulates as time goes on and the alcoholic gets sicker. Hiding becomes a way of life that goes unchallenged and unquestioned as the lives of those who keep the family secret are twisted, knotted, and distorted.

These children, when they grow up, still talk about how alone they feel. They are the victims of a double bind: They are still afraid to talk because they may reveal the secret; and remaining alone, they strengthen the very behavior that protects the secret—not talking. It is a circular trap, the kind you dream about in your most tortured nightmares.

It is much easier to deal with illness in which behavior is predictable: The anorexic doesn't eat; the child with poison ivy scratches; the psychopath lies; the lame limp; the seasick throw up. In alcoholism, nothing is predictable. At the same time, unpredictability is not something you can count on. And that is what makes it so excruciatingly confounding for children who are left in the dark as the family secret is fiercely guarded and all members join in the conspiracy of silence.

What Is Alcoholism?

"The biggest secret of all," says a man who is now an alcoholism counselor, "was inside me and how awful I felt deep down." Only in adulthood did he begin to understand how the disease, alcoholism, was behind much of the pain and turmoil in his life.

There is no simple definition of just what alcoholism is. When it comes to the most severe form, experts agree; but what lesser symptoms should be given the name is still debatable. For example, should problem drinkers—those whose lives are disrupted by their drinking—be called alcoholic? Some say yes, pointing out that if they are not yet addicted, chances are they soon will be. Dr. Morris Chafetz, the first director of the National Institute of Alcohol Abuse and Alcoholism, says bluntly: "Alcoholism is drinking too much, too often. It is permitting alcohol to play an inordinately powerful role in a person's life." The World Health Organization defines it more narrowly as "a pathological dependence on alcohol."

With this dependence (or physical addiction) come withdrawal symptoms—shaking, delirium tremens (d.t.'s), and other serious physical effects—when the drinking stops. With it also comes the development of tolerance so that the drinker needs more and more to get the same effect. As time goes on and the illness progresses, tolerance decreases until even a drink or two can produce intoxication. Perhaps because of the deterioration of liver or brain function, a small dose hits with the power of a large one.

The progression of the illness is often unnoticeable because it moves so slowly. In men, it is estimated that ten to twelve years elapse between early-stage problem drinking and full-blown alcoholism. In women, progression is telescoped. They start drinking later and move on more quickly to late-stage symptoms.

At this late stage alcoholism is usually recognizable as a chronic, relapsing disease. To understand what is really happening does not require an official diagnosis. The actress Mercedes McCambridge, a recovering alcoholic, looked back on her family and observed, "There is alcoholism on both sides of my family. They all died sober. They were all marvelous people. None of them found their way to Alcoholics Anonymous. They merely stopped drinking. What happened I don't know, because it was always hushed up. They all died of something nice." Ms. McCambridge herself finally had to acknowledge reality.

Alcoholism is "all hushed up." Claudia Black, a social worker who treats children of alcoholics, estimates that 40 percent grow up and leave home without ever being sure of the truth. They either don't know or deny what they know. A thin blond model, in treatment for her own alcoholism, is the only one in her family who sees her father as an alcoholic. It took her a long time to figure out that she learned to avoid him in the mornings because his need for a drink, not just plain bad temper, made him so moody that he would flare up and slap her around.

You may never have seen your parent drinking, or drunk, or at any rate drinking too much. And although drinking is blamed for everything in some families, you may not be sure it was alcohol that caused the trouble in yours. You may also have been too young or too protected. One woman says she didn't realize her parents were alcoholic until she was thirty-three years old. "I was tuned out. My whole childhood is a blank. I didn't feel like part of the human race. I didn't feel at all. The hate and fighting were so never ending that it took all these years for me to begin to face what went on and what was behind it. When I finally remembered one incident—my mother, drunk, pouring hot oatmeal over my hand—the whole picture began to come together."

Like this suburban mother, most alcoholics don't fit the stereotype of the lying-in-the-gutter drunk. They work, raise families, serve in the military, teach children. They are every place, and it is estimated that one in ten Americans who drink become alcoholic. Set in opposition to the skid-row stereotype is the romantic view of the alcoholic as genius. Look at the playwright Eugene O'Neill and the actress Vivien Leigh. But critics agree that no one wrote better or acted better because of alcohol, and the drug does not augment talent. What it may do is lower inhibitions so that a person *seems* to be doing better, or it may make it easier for someone who is very tense to relax enough (at first) to write or paint or act. In the end, though, because it is a central nervous system depressant, it interferes with performance of all kinds. It slows reaction time, blurs vision, and impairs judgment.

Alcohol also induces bewildering personality changes—a quiet person may become boisterous or violent; a happy one may become sad, crying for what seems like no reason at all. In the long run it is implicated in the development of throat cancer, heart disease, cirrhosis of the liver, and mental deterioration, among other serious conditions. It is involved in an estimated 25 percent to 50 percent of all hospital and mental hospital admissions.

It almost always interferes with parenting. The alcoholic is "not there" in some way. He or she is "out to lunch," "spaced out," "AWOL," "on the road," or whatever you want to call it. And it isn't because the parent sometimes isn't there physically or doesn't come home that children feel unsafe. Even when the parent is there, he or she can't listen, doesn't hear, or misinterprets what is said. When they are not heard or are misunderstood over and over again, children react with despair, anger, or fear, feeling vulnerable and doubting their very existence. And those emotions are at the very core of the life of a child who lives with someone who is drinking too much. One alcoholism counselor put it succinctly. He said he had gone through his childhood feeling like shouting at his mother, "Life is in session. Are you present?"

The Cover-up

Deception begun at home permeates the neighborhood and the community. Friends don't talk to friends. They look the other way rather than acknowledge the drinking. People laugh and make sick jokes about drunks and drunkenness. Other people blame poverty, lack of education, poor parenting, ethnic and racial origins for the drinking. As society is embarrassed by what is happening and refuses to look at it, the family living with alcoholism becomes more and more isolated. The pact of silence intensifies the disgrace, which is part of what made the hiding necessary in the first place.

In some families the other side of the big secret is the sympathy seeker, the martyr—usually the wife—who carps incessantly to neighbors and relatives about her plight. Her complaints are conspiratorial, designed to line up allies in her never ending struggle to justify her own point of view and keep up appearances. She is often the only one who does talk while she warns the rest of the family to say nothing. Like many other children of alcoholics you may never have talked outside your immediate family circle about the drinking.

Corinne, whose mother always kept their apartment spotless,

even when she was working full time, says that she doesn't know to this day whether neighbors in her building knew about her father's drinking. She is like the nearsighted nudist who takes off her glasses before she takes off her clothes so that others won't see her. The members of the alcoholic's family believe that they are hiding the problem from everyone, but the reality is that everyone else can see.

Corinne's father was a binge alcoholic who would disappear for weeks at a time and then reappear with no explanation as to where he had been or why he had been gone so long. No one ever saw him drunk or drinking at home or in the neighborhood. She pretended to herself and friends, too, that he was "away on business" and would announce triumphantly to schoolmates that her father had returned with lots of wonderful presents. Of course they would never be shown or shared because they were imaginary. The fact that they didn't exist didn't matter; hiding the truth was the important thing.

This is a peculiar quirk that hangs on in alcoholic families. It is as if the hiding is a habit that necessitates ignoring the realities. The person who needs to behave surreptitiously does so no matter what the objective or current situation. It is possible that this pattern of behavior stems from the nature of alcoholism itself. One man who had been sober for many years looked out the window, saw a friend walking up to the front door, and without really thinking, slipped his glass of ginger ale under his easy chair. Another young man told his wife, when she asked, that the insurance payments had been made. In fact, they had not. There was nothing to lose by telling the truth, for her question was intended only to gather information. But the man lied as he had heard his father do so many times when it came to money. Secrecy, evasion, and deception all became as acceptable as the truth.

This lesson, learned in childhood, is reinforced when family members don't discuss honestly what is happening. The result is that everyone becomes suspicious and angry. With little outlet for these emotions, people become lonely islands, and honest communication ceases to exist. There are no hugs, no acknowledgments of sharing, no feelings of mutual support and love, but, instead, interminable friction, distrust, and skepticism. Secrets inevitably give rise to jealousy too. And then there is more secretiveness, embarrassment, guilt, fighting, distancing, and isolation. A child cannot explain all this to himself so he continues to feel unsafe in the very setting in which he should feel most protected.

What Is Real?

There is so frequently a discrepancy between what they are told is happening and what is actually going on that children of alcoholics are not sure of what they see, what they hear, and what they feel. In other words, they don't believe their own perceptions.

This lack of self-trust often stems from trying to make things right in order to feel safe and then being puzzled and frustrated at not succeeding. Thus, a small child will deny his own experience in order to validate a parent. Why does this happen? What does it accomplish? One adult daughter of an alcoholic mother answered, "This is how I see it: All children require love, protection, and guidance as they develop. That was true of me and so I did what I could to make it seem as if my mother was really okay and then I would feel safe. And the way I did it was to deny the worth or reality of my own experience, and I became very good at that. I tried to make things look as if I had parents behaving like parents. No child wants to be without a parent. The basic problem with my either/or thinking was that when it made my parent right, it made me wrong. And the converse was true too. When it made me right, then my parent must have been wrong. So a continual struggle-of-war took place. Who was right? Who was wrong? What was really happening? Where should the blame lie? No wonder I'm still bewildered."

For some, early experiences with a parent who is having blackouts may account for difficulty in distinguishing real from unreal. A blackout is a memory loss caused by the continual action of alcohol on the brain. It is not deliberate and may not be observable. The drinker doesn't pass out or lose consciousness, but simply has no way of recalling what happened during a short or even a fairly long period of time. (*The Lost Weekend,* a classic book subsequently made into a movie, vividly depicts an alcoholic blackout.) A man may come home and ask his drinking wife if there have been any phone calls for him. She glibly answers, "No." But, in fact, only ten minutes earlier the child heard his mother on the phone with someone who was clearly asking to speak to his father.

The child is puzzled, but doesn't dare ask about it because he has been rebuffed so many times for questioning. By now he has begun to doubt the evidence of his own eyes and ears. Was there really a phone call? Is his mother lying? Did she forget? The truth is she is not lying; she never knew. The phone call wasn't locked into place in her memory bank so she could retrieve it later. But how can a child understand this?

Even when a parent does not have blackouts, inconsistencies and mixed messages give rise to confusion. The child is told one thing and something else happens. He is told everything is fine, but he sees that it isn't fine at all. Mom says she has never felt better and soon goes and vomits in the toilet. Dad rages at his boss, quits his job, and says he didn't need the work anyway. But the next day he is saying that there isn't going to be enough money for food and they should all tighten their belts. The family's insistence that everything is all right and everyone healthy in the face of the realities is what is so perplexing.

As the child goes on failing the "environment test," seeing what no one else around him seems to see, he wonders if he is out of his mind. The inability to trust his own feelings and perceptions puts him in a precarious position. Trying to do away with uneasiness by hiding it and hoping that no one else will see is exhausting. But this way, a big part of the family secret remains intact.

The Fighting

You probably remember the quarreling that went on at home. Chances are that whether the arguments were about who was supposed to feed the dog or where the money was going to come from to pay the rent, the source of the friction was unimportant. The important thing was that it was always there.

Like the drinking, the quarreling had to be hidden or excused as "bad temper" or "a loud kid" in case an outsider wondered about the noise. No matter what the fighting was about, children interpret it (and the drinking) as their fault. Children look inside themselves for solutions and when the drinking is out of control, they spontaneously conclude that they are to blame.

One woman remembers lying in bed listening to her parents' voices booming through the bedroom wall. She was certain the arguments had to do with her weight, no matter what the reality was. Even when she had clear evidence that the fights had nothing to do with her, she continued to believe that "maybe I could have stopped the arguments if only I had been thinner."

These fights were verbal. But when there is drinking it is likely that some arguments will escalate to violence or even become life threatening. A man who grew up in the South with an alcoholic father whose family routinely toted shotguns remembers the time his father used him for target practice. The neighbors ignored the noise, thinking it was just those crazy brothers having a little too much to drink again and raising hell. The boy survived because his father's aim was shaky, but he spent nights cowering under the covers, expecting every parental argument (which he felt he had caused) to be punishable by death. In cases like this, families need legal recourse and police protection.

The fighting is not always loud or violent. Just as often it is silent, seething, grudging anger—a quiet closing of doors, leaving the room, turning away, "Nobody yelled in my family," a doctor says. "It was more subtle but just as terrifying."

The conflict is not necessarily confined to parents. Children may take it out on one another, too, for when there is not enough parental love and attention to go around, they vie with one another for what there is. As children watch their parents, they see them provoking each other, arguing, harassing, bickering, complaining, and adopt these ways. It is no wonder many grow up with battling as second nature and carry on the family tradition of discord.

There are some families in which the children stick closer together in reaction to parental fighting. "My sister was my best friend," says one woman. "We hid in the attic together when my father was on a rampage. And we still look out for each other."

Fears

Almost all children of alcoholics describe the fear with which they returned home from school or a visit to a neighbor, overwhelmed with apprehension because they could not be sure what would greet them as they opened their own front doors. Mothers were just as likely to be there sprawled out on the floor as they were to be there with open arms and a welcoming smile. Fathers might still be at work, but there was always the chance that they hadn't gotten to work that day and would be home drunk and ready for a fight. Children learn how to save themselves from overt embarrassment. They learn to manipulate the environment to keep the peace, and they learn early not to take the added risk of bringing a friend home to face what could turn out to be a social and emotional calamity.

Most children have been taught not to "snitch" and they see talking about or exposing their parents' problems as some sort of betrayal. And with alcoholism, there's no telling what will happen at home if the word gets out that a child has been talking. The potential price is too high. A social worker who now works with young children has never revealed that she grew up in an alcoholic home. "I can't talk about it. I'm too scared. My parents said not to."

There is another very practical reason for not talking about the drinking. "I told my friend that my father threw all his shoes out the window last night when he was drinking and she told her mother. Now she can't play with me any more." The isolation of the alcoholic family is always increased when outsiders feel insecure or threatened by rumors. They stay away to protect themselves from what might happen or what they imagine *could* happen.

What could happen adds to the uneasiness of the children in the family itself. Like most people, they have deep fears about the future. "What if something happens? Who will take care of me? What if someone gets sick or dies? What if there is a car crash or the house catches fire?" These fears can be real and vivid for anyone, but for the child living where someone is drinking too much the fears are well founded; catastrophes are more imminent and more likely.

Even without major crises. "There was no light at the end of the tunnel where I lived. It was black all the way," says one son of an alcoholic father. It is this nonstop quality, the interminable, unrelenting anxiety that is so powerful. And it persists whether the child is in or out of the house, young or grown up.

Disappointments

Ivan had two alcoholic fathers. The first was his natural father, the second his mother's new husband. His "real" father lived in a nearby town and called one day to tell twelve-year-old Ivan that his grandmother had died and he planned to take him to the funeral. He said he would pick him up the next afternoon. Ivan was upset by his grandmother's death, for she had taken special care of him when he was little. Since his parents' split-up two years earlier, he hadn't seen her, but he still felt very attached.

He waited alone on the porch for his father to come. His mother stayed inside, still angry and unsympathetic toward her ex-husband, who, she had heard, was still drinking. Ivan's father never came. Confronted by his son years later, he gave a lame excuse—he had sent a friend to pick him up, but the friend had not been able to find the house.

Disappointments like this come from all sides. Mom has promised an early dinner so the family can go to the movies, but dad, out drinking, doesn't turn up on time. They don't get to eat early enough and are late for the movie. Mom is seen as the villain, the one who broke the promise. Or dad has said he will take everyone on a boat ride. Mom is "too sick" to go. As it turns out, the whole family has to stay home because dad doesn't dare leave his wife alone. He can't trust her. She might start a fire with her incessant smoking. To the children, he is the one who didn't keep his word.

When unpredictability results in disappointment after disappointment, it finally gets the children down. As they grow older they may blot out the disturbing incidents, but they never forget the uneasy feeling tone. It makes little difference whether the disillusionments are emotionally laden (as they were in Ivan's case) or relatively trivial—a trip to the store is canceled, a walk to the mailbox is postponed, a promised cupcake isn't there when the lunch box is opened. Children are upset over and over again. And, true to the family tradition of secrecy, they keep their distress to themselves. Eventually, they stop expecting what they have been promised because they have been let down too often. They've been betrayed by both parents so consistently that as adults they anticipate disappointment in both casual and intimate relationships. The longing for consistent care and nurturing seems to go on and on, so they continue to search for the mother and father they never had. And they remain children to their peers, which in turn blocks or hampers any mature relationship they may attempt.

Growing Up Too Fast

At the same time, children who live with a parent who drinks too much are forced to grow up too fast. Here's what Robin has to say:

"I guess I was about twelve. I remember I was shoved out of bed by my sister, who rolled over suddenly and pushed me onto the floor. I knew I wasn't supposed to awaken our parents and I was supposed to do my chores before they got up.

"I remember shivering in the kitchen and wishing I were back in bed. But that would mean being pushed out again. It was up to me to get out the breakfast cereal and put the milk on the table for the others. I turned on a big pot of water for tea and then I was awake enough to remember the uniforms.

"We would be severely reprimanded by our teachers if our clothing was wrinkled or spotted. I was careful that morning not to burn my fingers. I went through the motions of pressing the three uniforms and three pairs of pants and shirts so I could at least say I had done it no matter what shape the clothing finally took. As I ironed, I could hear arguing in our parents' bedroom. I closed my ears by humming to myself.

"I yelled, 'Get dressed!' counting on the inevitable hubbub to drown out the harsh bedroom voices. The others came in, grabbed their uniforms, and went scurrying to ready themselves for school. There wasn't enough milk to go around; I had forgotten to stop for it the day before. That morning some had to have their cereal dry; they complained, but there was nothing I could do then. I would pick up more in the afternoon on my way home.

"Why do I remember that morning? It was no different from any other. But now I think it was the beginning of the realization that I was the mother and father in our family even though I wasn't the oldest and my sister should have been taking some of the responsibility, too. I don't know what would have happened to us if I hadn't done what I did. But it never made me feel good; I felt put-upon and anxiety-ridden. Now I'm furious that I missed my childhood."

Saul, too, is seething with resentment. He was forced to take over at home before he was tall enough to reach the cups that hung in the cupboard above the sink. He remembers one morning in particular when his little brother, then two, was crying for his morning milk. While their mother slept he decided to calm the little boy by getting the drink for him. He climbed into the sink and grabbed the cup off its hook, but he lost his grip and it crashed to the floor. So that his mother wouldn't find out, he tried to clean up the mess by pushing the broken pieces under a nearby cabinet. A sharp piece cut the back of his hand. As his little brother became more and more hysterical, he too began to cry. But he had already learned that it was futile to try to awaken his mother and that even if he succeeded, he would only be scolded for getting her up. His memory of that morning fades as he recalls looking at the blood on his hand. Like many other memories of his early years, there are snatches and pieces, most with resolutions omitted.

As he looks back, however, other partial pictures emerge like snapshots to remind him now of how much responsibility he was forced to take and how guilty he felt right from the start because he was not able to live up to his parents' expectations. Once he closed the storm window on his finger—he was trying to be the "man" of the family. Another time he hid the car keys from his mother. He knew she wasn't supposed to drive because once, when his father still lived at home, he had heard him telling her that she couldn't have the keys. But he didn't quite understand why she wasn't supposed to use the car. He doesn't remember hiding the keys so much as the pain on the back of his legs as his mother hit him with the broom handle in response to what he thought was "acting grown up." He nevertheless continued to feel compelled to take on what he then saw as his responsibilities.

When he remembers the times he watched the older kids in the neighborhood play baseball, more resentment rises up. They were preparing themselves for the "big leagues," they told him. He watched wistfully, with a fleeting wish to be included. But he quelled the wish and rationalized the exclusion by telling himself that they were "babyish" and that he had more important, "manly" things to take care of at home. And he would leave, dragging his feet, hiding his weeping, numbed to the internal conflict.

Another young man, now in his thirties, says he had to grow up too rapidly when he was forced at the age of nine to take the place of his father, who died of alcoholism. As a child, he hadn't minded acting like a man. He felt good when his mother praised him for carrying the groceries in and running errands. But when he grew up he realized what he had missed. He was furious at his father for dying, at his mother for leaning on him so heavily, and at his sister for going her own way with pets and friends and not doing anything to help. Now he feels he has to make up for what he didn't have, so instead of acting like a mature adult, he fails to pay bills, stays out all night, speeds erratically on a motorcycle (he could easily afford a car), and generally lives like an experimenting adolescent. His attempts to recapture the youth he didn't have now interfere with his work (he can't keep his eyes open during the day) and with his relationships with women, one of whom he inadvertently heard characterize him as "awfully silly for a grown man."

His ability to mature was somehow stunted by his forced early growth; now he has trouble sharing with and giving to others, although he keeps trying to please them in order to get longed-for approval. When the approval is not forthcoming, he is crushed and furious. The anger stems from a time when he had to take care of his mother.

Not only are many children of alcoholics put in charge of younger brothers and sisters; their drinking parents also need them for physical care and emotional support, which includes listening, comforting, and approving. They become, in effect, the parents of their parents; their efforts shield the family's disorganization from prying eyes. But when these children grow up they feel short-changed, as if they had missed something they deserved, and they continue to struggle to get what they didn't have. They find themselves, in their thirties and forties, still "pseudo-adults," not totally or solidly mature, because they never had the opportunity to be children. Some find they haven't learned how to play, and they don't understand frivolity. They misinterpret the levity of others, which in turn makes them feel even more "out of it." One young man said, "When I see my own kids play, it's as though I've never seen anything like it before. I feel like an anthropologist discovering a new tribal rite. Becoming a grownup before you're a kid isn't fair—I was robbed!"

Incest

If she grows up too fast, a girl will often replace her alcoholic mother, preparing food for a party or picking up a younger brother or sister at day care. She may replace her mother in another, more treacherous way too. A father came into the kitchen in which his wife and daughter were sitting and said, "Hi, honey. How does my tie look?" His wife began to answer, but the question was really directed to his daughter, who was replacing her mother emotionally in her father's life. When a woman is alcoholic and is unable or unwilling to be an adequate wife, her husband can easily turn to female children for companionship, comfort, and even sex. Incest does not occur only during drinking sprees, although there are active alcoholics who, when drinking, lose both their sense of propriety and their inhibitions. It is during such times that a man is most likely to approach a daughter. However, incestuous activity, even when there is drinking, cannot be entirely blamed on the drunk person, for the child who is accosted may unknowingly play a role in what actually happens. She may long for the closeness and affection that she missed or that had been offered so sparingly, and may invite her father's advances. Also, some women who lose interest in their husbands because of their drinking yet stay in the marriage actually permit a daughter to take over.

Thus incest is a way individuals adjust within a "family system." Needless to say, this is a sick way for a family to operate, and the effects, both immediate and long term, are consistently injurious. Many of the psychological consequences are similar to those of alcoholism. They include feelings of loss of control or worthlessness, and an overwhelming dependency on absolute secrecy.

When there is incest in an alcoholic family, it is the biggest secret of all and forces the cloak of concealment to tighten. It not only adds to the guilt associated with the drinking but serves to separate and isolate the family even more. And pressure from society reinforces the hiding, so that few people realize how frequently daughters of male alcoholics are sexually assaulted, not only by their fathers, stepfathers, or brothers, but also by their half-brothers, brothers-in-law, uncles, cousins, adoptive fathers, and grandfathers. Nor are most people aware that, even though it is relatively infrequent, incest takes place between adult women and male children.

Even though there are between 12 and 15 million victims among American women, according to estimates made by the American Psychological Association, many people, even those who have been victims of it, don't know what incest is. The accepted definition is "any sexual activity (intimate physical contact that is sexually arousing) between nonmarried members of a family." According to Blair and Rita Justice in their book *The Broken Taboo,* "Incestuous activity may be oral-genital relations, mutual masturbation, fondling and caressing erogenous areas of the body, or actual intercourse."

Statistics concerning alcoholism and incest are still hard to come by. But of the forty female incest victims interviewed by Dr. Judith Lewis Herman for her book *Father-Daughter Incest,* more than a third "considered their fathers to be problem drinkers." Dr. Herman points out that, "in childhood, fear usually overcomes any hope of relief; most girls dread discovery of the incest and do not reveal it to anyone outside the family."

It may stay unspoken inside the family too. "My father hid pornographic books under the mattress," says the daughter of an alcoholic. "My brother would pull them out and read them. From the books he got the notion that he and I should be a couple and that we should sleep together too. He was expected to look after me when our parents went out, but that's when he would force me to stay in his bed with him. I was frantic and guilty about his sexual advances, but I didn't know what to do about what was going on. I tried to escape by locking my bedroom door. But when my parents came home and found the door locked, they would punish me. I never told them why."

Another woman said, "I remember two times when my father was drunk and he started kissing me all over. I never told my mother because I knew she would be horrified; and she might not even believe what I told her. Now we're very close, but I would never tell her about that."

A woman asked her therapist if what had gone on between her and her father was really incest—she wasn't sure. Each time he was alone in the house with her, she said, her father opened his fly and showed her his penis. He told her that he wanted her to learn what a penis looked like, for there were no other males in the household, and he encouraged her to "feel" it and take a close look. Most of the time there was no physical contact between them, but he clearly took pleasure from "instructing" her repeatedly. Eventually her father asked her to bring home her girlfriends so he could "teach" them too, but soon she began to worry that one of them might tell about what was going on. The secret was never actually told, and this young woman had to learn from her therapist years later that, yes, this was incest. Only then was she finally able to reveal what she had been afraid to talk about all the time. She thought that if she talked it might cause her father to be sent to jail, lead to a divorce, or make both her parents desert her. So the secret was kept, no matter what the cost, as it is in so many families. And even though most states have mandatory reporting laws with penalties attached, incest remains a dark secret.

"My client is a victim of sexual abuse from her father. It went on for many years," a social worker reports. "She is one of three sisters, all brought up in a home where people rarely talked about what was on their minds. I asked my client if her sisters had gone through the same suffering; she said she absolutely had no idea and was somewhat surprised that I had asked. I suggested that she ask her sister, who lived nearby, and then come back and tell me. Yesterday she came bursting into my office. 'Shit, man, they had it too!' Yet this was a family with such a sense of Victorian propriety that when the mother went to the store she asked the butcher for 'chicken chests.' "

It happens all too frequently that when one daughter, the incest victim, moves out of the house, another daughter is chosen as the father's favorite. Sometimes all this goes on as the mother tacitly agrees to it or makes no move to protect her children. Like alcoholism, incest has intergenerational patterns and is passed down from mother to daughter—a colluding mother may herself have been a victim of incest. Paradoxically, however, in some families the complicity involved when and if the secret is shared keeps the family together, for if people attempt to divulge it, they sometimes find out, in addition to the shame, that people don't want to hear or believe them. The social worker went on: "If I hadn't asked my client to question her sister, she might never have discovered that the others had also been abused. The incest had been doing irreparable damage to each of them for years, and in all three it had led to passivity and/or promiscuity, which in turn resulted in self-hatred and shame. One sister could not, in spite of repeated efforts, make a successful heterosexual liaison. She has had two husbands and now lives alone with her two little boys, one by each man. My patient and the other sister are Lesbians, but un-happy with their choice and not able to establish lasting relation-ships either."

Incest victims are understandably conflicted. They both long to reveal their secret and, at the same time, are afraid to talk about it. The case here may explain the alacrity with which the long-held intimate details were shared with the social worker. The three women, even after they had left home, had never exchanged confidences, so they never realized the others were "getting it too."

Incest is probably the most difficult situation that children can have to live through. All feel the effects of their childhood experi-ence for a lifetime. Like a third-degree burn, it leaves a permanent scar. One woman says, "I feel intrinsically bad no matter what I do—no matter how good I am, the bad will come out."

Abuse

Children of alcoholics suffer other kinds of abuse as well; often it is life-threatening. Alcohol releases such violence, particularly in men, that a man who is drinking may not be conscious of his strength and can unwittingly injure his own children. Children have been hit or beaten just because they were in the wrong place at the wrong time or because they were trying to protect a mother or younger brothers or sisters. (One alcoholic man asked the court to remove his children from the household and put them in a fos-ter home because he was afraid of what he might do to them.)

It is officially estimated that drinking is involved in 38 percent of all child abuse cases, but this number represents only the tip of a huge iceberg. When abuse is denied or unremarkable in terms of immediate consequences, it is difficult for authorities, outsiders, or even close relatives to detect. In one middle-class family three lit-tle girls were expected to spend Sundays visiting their grandpar-ents. Their alcoholic mother dressed them carefully in their best dresses with hair bows to match and, at the same time, hurried them on by repeatedly hitting them with the back of her hairbrush when they didn't move fast enough. As they went out the door stifling their sobs, she warned them not to breathe a word about the preparations. Several times they had left the house with blood on their white socks and were told to tell their grandma that they "fell."

The game of pretending everything is fine includes many ways of denying the terrible reality of physical abuse. "We never hit you," the husband of an alcoholic told his son, who remembered the black-and-blue lumps. "What are you making such a fuss about? You're making it all up. Everybody has troubles in life, and yours were no worse than any other kid's." When he went off to college, this young man knew something was terribly wrong as his moods swung from deep depression to high elation, but he didn't know what the trouble was. At the student health service the counselor asked, "Are you flunking?" He said no, he was getting A's as usual. "Are you having trouble making friends?" He said he was generally well liked. "There's no reason, then, for you to take up my time. You're fine," the counselor reassured him. Later, still diagnosed as "fine," the young man had to screech for help by attempting suicide.

It is only years after the event itself that people talk about having been locked in closets, deprived of food, whipped, burned, or brutalized in some way. Even though physical punishment can be devastating, sometimes the suspense can be even worse than the actuality. The same young man recalled: "I knew that if my father was there when I got home, I'd get it in the neck. That walk home was terrifying. Something was going to happen and it would be awful and my imagination went wild. I could nearly feel my fingernails being pulled out and my nose being bashed in." When he got home he was often beaten, but he said and did nothing in his own defense. Like others who would rather suffer than be stranded for life with crippling guilt, he preferred being victimized than actively fighting back against or challenging his parent.

Neglect

Neglect is the absence of caring. The "not paying attention" is pervasive. "When I came downstairs in the morning," one man recalls, "there'd be my dad on the floor, usually with his head resting on the bottom step. I'd just step over him, go make my lunch, and leave for school. I expected it to be that way and I accepted it.

I didn't know how different it was in other people's families. And my mom never said anything. It was as if she didn't notice him. She probably didn't notice a lot of other things either."

When a parent, particularly a mother, is "not paying attention," neglect is inevitable. Teeth don't get brushed, hair is left unwashed, nails are not trimmed, bathing is haphazard, and clothing is inadequate or inappropriate. But lack of physical care may be just the beginning of general neglect. "I never had shoes that fit," a woman who is now an artist says. "They were always too big or too small. And sometimes I went to school wearing shorts when it was freezing outside. Nobody at home paid any attention. My mother made lasagna with raw pasta and dished up rice that had been dipped in water but not cooked—and she forced us to eat it." This alcoholic mother slept through the mornings while her husband left extra early for work. The children had no medical or dental checkups except the cursory ones they received at school.

Physicians have found that children of alcoholics have illnesses that were ignored. If they had been treated or recognized earlier, the prognosis would have been better. Those illnesses include scoliosis and other skeletal problems, orthodontic abnormalities, and hereditary errors of metabolism, all of which, if identified early, can be less serious than if they are left unattended.

Doctors also find children of alcoholics who have gastrointestinal complaints, headaches, or asthma—all related to stress. Often these are incorrectly assessed because both parents and children deny that they are living in a state of siege; therefore doctors have very few cues to lead them to look for alcohol abuse in their patients. Many physicians, however, join the denial brigade: How can alcoholism exist in a family that has a steady breadwinner, lives in a nice house, and pays its bills? The stereotype of the alcoholic as someone in the gutter—and certainly not a woman—persists among professionals as well as the general public. Even when a professional recognizes that alcohol may be behind a child's problem, there is no guarantee that the child will get the help he or she needs, for more than likely no one at home will cooperate or carry out the doctor's suggestions.

A truck driver, now in his forties, recalls that when he was a little boy he was not allowed to see the school guidance counselor even when referred there by his teacher. The teacher described him as "a steaming tea kettle, the lid about to blow off." But his parents told him to say nothing about what was happening at home. The boy saw the police there almost nightly, trying to keep his drinking parents from slaughtering each other, but they flatly refused to let him see the counselor.

Children such as this may be affected in subtle ways. The inner destruction is just as devastating even though the scars are unseen. One woman talks about her father as a source of money and nothing more. Now, as an adult, she herself has developed a similar way of relating. When her friends need her for companionship or advice she doesn't trust herself to give them what they need. She responds by giving money and gifts. She is bothered about her own tendency to "pay people off" and continues, as her father did, to confuse money with love. Another woman whose mother was alcoholic remembers, "My mother was not a falling-down drunk. But I was at that awful period of adolescence when I desperately needed someone to talk to. I would pour out my heart at night, and the next day she wouldn't remember a thing I had said."

If emotional needs are neglected, so are basic training and learning. It is assumed, generally, that as children grow up they learn how to enter the adult world. But since so much time and energy in the alcoholic family are given over to the drinking and the drinker, the elementary tasks of parenting may never be accomplished. "When I moved into my first apartment and had to buy curtains and a rug, I developed a severe case of 'fear of furnishing,'" says one young woman. "I'm thirty-six years old now and I've still never taken the responsibility of fixing up my own place."

People who have been treated like "nothings" never see themselves as competent or able to cope on their own with ordinary, day-to-day living. But this is hard to recognize as neglect. Nothing shows. There are no scars—other than a bare living space or ill-fitting clothing. A young hairdresser says, "I was always ashamed of my clothes. My parents' attitude was, if I wanted it, it was no good. I still don't know how to pick out a decent dress for myself." However, one forty-year-old woman has finally gained some sense of self-esteem. She says, "Now, even if the cranberry jelly mold collapses, it's okay with me because I can chalk it up to bad luck rather than to someone's drunkenness or my own awkwardness."

Beyond the Secret

Abuse, neglect, and denial are not easy to overcome. Now that you've had a good look inside the house that guards the secret and have seen the reality beyond the front room, you may want to turn around and leave. It is neither a pretty nor a comforting picture, but it is an honest look at reality—a reality that may have been, a reality that may still be. And the possibility for change is there too, along with the hiding and the disorder. Alcoholics get well; families recover; children find out how to solve the twistogram of "Who am I? How did I get this way?" and go on to confident maturity.

2

Fantasyland: Surviving in the Family

> When I was a kid I would sit on a big rock outside
> and pretend that I was a princess in disguise and
> someday I would go back to my own country and
> live in a beautiful palace. I knew I didn't belong in
> this mess.
>
> Andrea, Age 23

One of the things that helps people reach some sort of mature equilibrium is an understanding of how they managed to survive the chaos of living in a family faced with alcoholism. Many found the key in their ability to use their imagination. Fantasies are not arbitrary; dreams (waking or sleeping) have meaning. They may lighten the burden by serving as an escape, they may have unconscious significance that is difficult to understand, or they may be used to explain the inexplicable.

If they serve as an escape, they are usually full of sunshine and happy endings; if they originate in the unconscious, they appear strange or difficult to believe, like wishing for the death of someone you love. And if they are explanations of the unknown, they help clarify the incomprehensible: "I wouldn't be having these problems if I had been born ten years later," or "If there had been more money we would have been happy."

In the lives of those who have lived with an alcoholic parent, fantasies that have to do with rescuing, recognizing reality, controlling, assigning blame, and trying to make understandable the deeply embedded myths that serve to deny what really is or was appear over and over again. Some fantasies are inventive ways to

25

cope. They help do away with feelings of impotence, of being different, of being out of control, worthless, or alone. Others are used in treatment as a route to understanding what happened. Some people are actually able to create a private world that gives them a way to escape from time to time so that they can keep from being pulled into the craziness.

Four Myths

There are four myths working behind the scenes in the lives of most children of alcoholics. Their power varies from person to person, but most people experience each of them at one time or another. They are what lie behind many of the fantasies.

1. I Caused the Alcoholism: I Should Do Something about It

It is not by accident that this myth comes first. It is probably the one held most widely and the one to which people cling most fervently. Very young children ("Mommy says that if I'm a good girl she will act nicer"), adolescents ("If I get better grades they won't fight so much and there will be less drinking"), and adults ("What did I do wrong?") all share it. It is the foundation on which guilt, blame, and struggles for autonomy rest. It leads inevitably to frustration and helplessness. Any individual enmeshed in a rescue fantasy, believing that he or she can make a difference (particularly to the progression of alcoholism), ultimately feels blocked and unneeded. A young college student recalls that when he was a little boy he saved all his pennies, convinced that if he could buy his mother a bottle of her favorite perfume she would be so pleased she would stop drinking. "Now I know better," he says sadly. But he is still trying to be the savior, imagining that when he finds the magic solution his parents will finally appreciate him.

The most difficult blow hits with the dismal realization that changes are impossible to maneuver and that the responsibility is not one's own. A young woman described the image that came to her when she thought about her alcoholic mother: "She was a real big balloon, the size of a room. And I was a tiny, two-inch hypodermic needle. I was trying to give her a transfusion that would save her but the more I gave, the more nothing happened."

Sometimes the wish to be the savior is tied up with the wish to be seen and respected. A man says of his alcoholic parents, "I used to imagine them noticing me and appreciating me. Again and again I'd see them smiling as I got some special sort of Boy Scout badge for rescuing people."

2. I'm Not Like Anyone Else

Right from the start, children who have lived with alcoholism feel their families are different, even though they don't know exactly how. They also feel different themselves or feel set aside as "different" by neighbors, friends, and relatives. They explain this by telling themselves:

"I was adopted."

"Somebody switched babies in the hospital and gave me to the wrong family."

"I'm really a Martian. I came from outer space."

The feeling of not belonging can be a reassuring one. It says, in effect, "I'm really okay, even if everyone else is mixed up." And it holds a kernel of hope that the mistake will be rectified and the child will go back to his or her rightful place. But the feeling of being marked as an oddity by the outside world is not so comforting. One man said he felt as if he wore a yellow armband and that everyone saw that he had been labeled, not a Jew (which he wasn't), but the son of an alcoholic mother and an atheist father. He also felt that he was watching the world from the outside, that he wasn't really a part of it. "Everything has a dreamlike quality for me," he says.

3. I Have to Be in Control of Myself and Everything Else or My World Will Fall Apart

One purpose of fantasy is to make the feeling of being out of control go away, at least temporarily. A fantasy is at the mercy of its owner. It can be manipulated and made to do what the owner needs it to do. It can be made to disappear and it can be brought back again. For children of alcoholics, that not only feels good, it feels *safe*.

A man who grew up near an amusement park remembers standing outside the gate and watching the rides when things got rough at home. "I used to imagine myself as the man who worked the merry-go-round," he says. "I would stop it and start it and collect the tickets. I felt like a big shot, and I didn't have to worry that any of the horses would start doing crazy things."

When fantasies arise from guilt, uncertainty, and fear, they sometimes only reinforce feelings of impotence and hopelessness. They are not, then, escapes or possible ways of solving current dilemmas; they are extra burdens. The woman who returns home to check on her parents' well-being believes she can control the situation simply by arriving on the scene. At the same time, she questions her ability to make a real difference, so she has to keep coming back. After a while she knows she has little say in what they do but she can't get herself to stop the visiting. She feels out of control herself and very foolish. One woman put it this way, " 'If only' is a very good way to give us the illusion that we have some control in our lives, especially in relation to our parents. If only I had the power to fix my parents; but I don't and I still blame that inadequacy on myself."

4. Someone Will Come Along or Something Will Happen That Will Change All This

This myth ("A fairy godmother will wave her wand") grows out of a feeling of impotence. It takes the blame away at last and puts it on an outside force. "If something magical can save me, something magical must have put the curse on us" is the unspoken explanation. It also offers hope, a welcome change from the other three major myths. But in the real world it does little to make things better. Families that wait for change feel that control is beyond them; they can't do anything about guiding their lives; they drift on waves that take them one way and then another according to the tides.

Sometimes the wait for the fairy godmother goes on for years. "I dream about a tall, dark, and handsome man and a house with a picket fence around it, but I don't know how to do anything that will make my wishes come true. I don't even know how to find a job so I can make money. Maybe my father will die and I'll inherit his money and then things will be better. My husband thinks he's going to win the lottery; we're both waiting." These two hang on to their dreams but they can't implement them. They simply hope that the day will come when something will be decided for them. Then the waiting, the abdication of control, the stagnation lead to ongoing depression.

Growing up means leaving the fictitious world behind. However, there are many people, including children of alcoholics, whose perceptions have been so distorted that they hold on to myths and fantasies that have long since ceased to be appropriate or useful. Some say the line between their dreams and reality is blurred and they can hardly tell what is real and what isn't. One confused young man says, "I wish things were back to normal. But the reality is that they never were normal; it's all make-believe."

These people may even feel that they themselves have no real existence. A social worker of many years says tearfully, "I feel, still, as if the claim check to my life was lost. One day, when I was a young teenager, there was a school holiday; my mother had to work. So I decided on my own to try an adventure and go to visit her in the office where she had worked for ten years. When I arrived I asked for her, telling the people who I was and why I had come. They looked at me incredulously. The fact was they didn't know that I existed. They didn't know my mother had children. I didn't exist. No one wanted to claim me."

Magical Thinking

This feeling of being nonexistent and essentially powerless is in sharp contrast to a child's early feelings of omnipotence. An infant cries and its mother materializes, as if by magic. Very young children continue to imagine they have enormous, frightening powers. Wishing something won't happen can stop it; wishing it will happen can make it take place. Doing one thing wrong can bring on a calamity. It is this kind of primitive thinking that is enshrined in the sidewalk rhyme "Step on a crack, break your mother's back."

As the child grows older, reality corrects these feelings of omnipotence. But the child in an alcoholic family may not talk much to other children or adults, and this isolation reinforces the early beliefs and keeps them from being corrected. The misleading information is further strengthened because the alcoholic rarely takes responsibility for his or her actions. The child is blamed as the easiest target, piling confirmation on the youngster's already distorted understanding.

A twelve-year-old girl (who normally would have been expected to give up magical thinking as she moved into adolescence) contemplated suicide when her father was taken to the hospital. She figured if she ended her own life she would also end all the trouble in her family.

Sometimes the wish is that the parent—not necessarily the alcoholic parent—will die. Then outsiders will pay more attention, will come to the rescue, will befriend the child, or will emerge as new, loving parents. But the sword is double-edged, for wishing for a parent's death and believing that wishes have the power to come true gives rise to guilt that doesn't go away easily. And wishing for a disaster while recognizing the possibility of the wished-for disaster coming to pass is terrifying.

Taking responsibility for events they really can't control is another common characteristic of children from alcoholic homes. If the water boils over, it's their fault, even if someone else put the pot on the stove. A young man who counsels teenage drug abusers says, "I can finally look back at my childhood and not feel that I was to blame or that I could have done something about what was happening. I used to be miserable when I thought about what happened when my mother was drinking. So I blocked it all out. But now I know that people have a right to have a past. I'd repressed good as well as bad."

Turning Inward

Another way of avoiding the past and the present is turning inward. As a woman who is now a doctor discovered, "I could shut out life lived at top volume by going down ten steps to our finished basement. There I sewed doll costumes while my mother and father yelled at each other. The dolls were my 'real' family, and the sewing machine drowned out the noise."

In an attempt to cope with physical violence one woman learned to run out of the house and walk the sand dunes for hours. "When I cut off what was going on outside (that is, the blows) and went inside, there was God. He always made me feel better."

Daydreams helped a bright young man feel better. During high school and college he would climb into a tree and just let his mind float. But he barely scraped by academically and now he says, "What a waste."

One form of fantasy that may not be a waste has helped many young children survive hardships. When living with a parent who drinks too much becomes unbearable, some turn to imaginary companions. Here is the story of one such fantasy friendship:

At the age of five and a half, when Meg Rhynne's father lost his job and her mother went to work full time, Meg created her best friend, Fee Fee May Mays. Immediately she was dissatisfied with the name and changed it to Desdemona. Desdemona had a home of her own, down the street. But she spent nearly all her time at the Rhynnes'. Whenever she went home, Meg went along.

At the Rhynnes' the two girls always sat next to each other in the living room, at the table, on the floor with crayons, or sometimes on the front steps. They took baths together, slept together, and stared out the window together. Away from the house they were inseparable too. Desdemona rode next to Meg in the car; she stayed close to her in shopping centers, at the beach, and on the sidewalk near the house. Most important of all, they walked to school together, noticing other children walking in the same direction; they sat in the same chair in the classroom. They read the same read-alone books and held hands when questioned by their teacher, Miss Dowd. In the playground they stood together next to the fence watching the children play.

After school, on the walk home, they passed by Desdemona's house and decided whether or not to stop off there. Desdemona's mother and father were always home except when they went out to buy new clothing, cake and ice cream, or things for the house. The house was filled with soft couches and chairs and springy beds. There were fuzzy blankets, velvety carpets, and plenty of hiding places. Seven kittens, who never ended their kittenhood, followed the girls from room to room. Rays of sunlight filled every corner.

Meg's peculiar habits made her the butt of a great deal of teasing from her two brothers. Sometimes they became annoyed with her because she wouldn't listen to them, wouldn't pay attention to their games when they needed her, and would whisper to herself so they couldn't hear what she was saying. Sometimes she smiled to herself, but wouldn't share the joke with the boys.

They were puzzled because she would sit on one side of her chair, never in the middle. Sometimes she would even fall over onto the floor. When she sat down, she never faced the room or table in front of her. Instead, she held her face to one side, often nodding her head up and down. At meals she would ask for an extra piece of bread or a sweet dessert, then leave them on her plate. Sometimes she put the extras on a plate next to her own. Her brothers didn't mind this since they were delighted to get any leftovers for themselves.

Meg's mother didn't take the strange behavior so lightly. She worried about the odd, repetitive acts the little girl clung to so tenaciously. She particularly noted the look of terror on Meg's face when the rituals were interrupted. One time she forced her to sit in the center of her chair, but then Meg behaved even more strangely, leaning over the side and peering down at the floor, muttering the whole time and looking very frightened.

Meg's fantasy playmate served as a healthy outlet, a way to cope in an impossible situation. Her father, who drank heavily, vented his fury by lashing out at his children with the back of his hand. By the time Meg was fourteen, he was out of the house, and eventually he became a street derelict. But before he left, Meg's mother did little to protect the children from his wrath, even though she tried in other ways to make life normal for them. At the same time, she was well aware of their suffering. As the child of an angry alcoholic herself, she was too frightened to take things in hand effectively and never sought protection for herself or her children. She had been beaten up too many times. She coped by continuing to deny and by pretending that all was well.

Meg's Desdemona fantasy was a highly successful way for her to block out the family misery. It provided her with constant, nonthreatening companionship; it prevented the horror scenes that might have taken place had she brought a real friend home; and it gave her an ever-present person with whom she could share her thoughts, wishes, fears—and even her food!

The end of the Desdemona fantasy came quite suddenly. It was a simple matter for Meg to wipe Desdemona out. She just explained the disappearance to herself by imagining that Desdemona had died of a fall from an upper-story window and that the rest of the family and the house had been swept away in a sudden flood. As she put it, "The family, the fantasy, was one, two, three, gone—zero."

The end of Desdemona coincided with the beginning of Meg's own drinking. By the age of fifteen she had discovered a new way to blot out the world. She had become addicted to alcohol and no longer needed the fantasy.

Perhaps a positive aspect of Meg's dream world was that she was able to get rid of it when she didn't need it any more. The tragedy is, of course, that her replacement was such a dangerous one.

J. D. Salinger's story "Uncle Wiggly in Connecticut" tells of two college friends who talk, reminisce, and get drunk on an icy afternoon. One has a daughter, Ramona, who has an imaginary friend named Jimmy Jimmereeno. The Salinger story is so similar to the story of Meg that it becomes clear that where there is drinking there is a universality in the ways children find to escape.

Child psychiatrists say that it is the quality and the extent of the fantasy that are significant in determining when make-believe worlds begin to impinge upon and distort reality. When the child completely, or partially, leaves the real world behind and becomes submerged in an imaginary one, psychopathology begins and there is likely to be trouble. It is not that the fantasies themselves are unusual, weird, different, or sick; they are the common dreams that human beings share. Only when they take the place of reality and result in immobilizing the individual rather than making him or her freer do they become dangerous. It is then that the ability to control life is diminished rather than enhanced.

3

Merry Christmas
and Other Disasters

For as long as I can remember, I've been hoping
for the perfect Christmas. When I was a teenager
I thought things would be better in my twenties.
And then I thought it would happen when I hit
thirty. Every year I think it's going to be different,
and it never is. Here I am, practically middle-
aged, and nothing has changed.

John, Age 38

One reality of childhood is that very little of it is under the
child's control. Life is planned—or disrupted—by grown-
ups. The fantasy that holidays will be happy times conflicts
with the often sad reality that nothing a child can do will keep him
or her from feeling wretched.

Debbie grew up dreading holidays and birthdays and wed-
dings, all occasions when good things were supposed to happen
and bad things inevitably did. There was the Christmas her father
was supposed to be Santa and didn't come home at all. Then there
was the Christmas he did come home but got mad because he
didn't like the presents he'd been given, shoved them aside, then
locked himself in his room and "got loaded." There was her graduation from college. She was the first person in her family to make
it that far, and her father said he was proud. He promised he
wouldn't drink but he arrived for the ceremony roaring drunk
"and made an ass out of himself."

You, too, may remember your wish that "everything would be
like a Norman Rockwell painting" and your disappointment when
the day was ruined. Even today Debbie is waiting for the miracle
to happen. Her mother still clings to her with fierce determina-

34

tion; Debbie tries to shake her loose. Although her father died years ago, the family pattern hasn't changed significantly. There is still the carping about his drinking; the complaints that she isn't as dutiful as she might be; the terrible feeling of foreboding that something will happen to wreck the day. Worst of all, Debbie is beginning to lose hope.

Holidays are a particularly stressful time, and even though most people look forward to them, they do it with some trepidation. For adult children of alcoholics, there is more than the usual anxiety because, historically, so much went wrong, so many hopes were smashed, and so many anticipated events didn't materialize.

Why are holidays and family celebrations so frequently an invitation to disaster, and what can be done to avoid repeating the old patterns? Special occasions are risky for many families, but they are more risky in families with an alcoholic parent because they conjure up repeated images of calamity. The forebodings are not just nameless, vague forms; they are shadows cast by vivid memories of what actually did happen. As one man put it when asked about his experiences, "Holidays? You mean hellidays, don't you?" (Freud would have understood. He used the term "alcoholidays" in the English translation of his *Basic Works* to illustrate the cleverness of the workings of the mind which telescoped the two significant words and made them one.)

Some of the things that make holidays joyful and special are the very things that turn them into "hellidays." First, the change in regular routines leaves room for behavior held in check by the demands of daily life. If father is getting drunk once a week, he will pick Christmas or Thanksgiving. From his point of view there is no better time. He doesn't have to work, he has learned to deal with emotional times by drinking, and he firmly believes that celebrating isn't real celebrating if he doesn't drink.

Then there are the expectations that have been inflated by the media, the culture, and the family. The possibility of disappointment is built in. The daughter of an alcoholic mother remembers the time the turkey didn't get cooked because her mother was drinking and forgot to defrost it. The tragedy was not that they went hungry, but that they had violated a tradition. They were clearly different from other families on their block and they knew it. "Thanksgiving and Christmas are supposed to be loving," she says, "but on holidays I felt like I was in the front line, fighting.

And Thanksgiving was a horror show until the guests arrived and took the heat off us. We were always wondering what unpredictable explosion would happen next. And we thought that everyone else in the world was having a great time." Of course, everyone wasn't; unrealistic expectations cause trouble at many dinner tables. But to insulated alcoholic families, the situation seems unique.

Such families are not unique, either, in the feeling of urgency that imbues every holiday or special event with excessive importance. "It's now or never," one woman explains. "There's only one Christmas or birthday or Thanksgiving a year, and it has to count! I've got to make it a good one; I may never have another chance."

The fear that there may never be another birthday or Christmas or Thanksgiving is based on a real possibility. Certainly no child walks around with statistics in his or her head; but the grim fact is that alcoholic men die earlier than those in the average population, and divorce is distressingly frequent. Even a child realizes that family life is precarious and so are important family occasions. The adult, then, is well aware that these occasions come loaded with associations from the past, usually sad ones, and are weighted down with the whole family's emotional investment. Maybe, the hope is, this time will be different if the effort is great enough. But the risks are there, and when the efforts fail the anguish, though expected, is hard to accept.

Some children of alcoholics work hard to make today's celebrations better than yesterday's. Others have just given up. A woman, now in her thirties, remembers the surprise party she and her mother planned one year for her older sister. They stayed up half the night baking a cake and decorating it with flowers and fruits. They hid it in the refrigerator (perhaps they should have known better), planning to unveil it the next afternoon when friends gathered in the backyard.

That morning her father started drinking. By noon no one else would get him a beer. Angry and half drunk, he rummaged in the refrigerator himself and the cake fell out onto the floor, ruined. He reacted with his usual "Don't worry," went downtown, and bought a garish, unpalatable replacement. The whole family project was undermined but he was oblivious and still drinking. In the midst of the outdoor celebration he began shoving the boyfriend of one of the girls, and the embarrassed couple left. The younger sister escaped to her room in tears. She resolved never to have a birthday party herself and she never has. It is almost as if her past were preserved in alcohol, like one of those anatomical specimens in biology class. She can't change it, of course, but she can't get at it and discard it either.

Whatever lesson she learned as a child seems to her the only one possible. But this isn't so. There are alternatives, and she doesn't have to spend the rest of her life abiding by the resolutions she made as a bewildered, hurt little girl. One therapist who believes behavior is learned and can therefore be unlearned puts it this way: "It doesn't have to take years to find your way out of the woods. Find someone who can show you the path others have used."

Bill, a middle-aged salesman, remembers Christmas as a time of uncertainty and dread, and he still feels that way. One year he asked for a recording of *Nutcracker Suite* (those were in the days of brittle 78 RPM records). He had recently discovered the public library as a refuge from the arguments at home and had heard the music there. In spite of the fact that money was scarce and getting something you really wanted was rare, his mother had bought it for him. Christmas afternoon his drunken father sat down hard on the record, which had inadvertently been left on his chair. "What the hell is this?" said his father. He got up and then went on drinking. The recognition of his father's blatant insensitivity combined with a sense of his own vulnerability marked a turning point in Bill's life. To this day he doesn't expect much and is Scrooge-like and scathing on the subject of holidays. Presents, he says, are a sham.

Other people have the opposite reaction. For them, presents have exaggerated importance. They need to receive them to be reassured that they are loved. And with presents, love can safely be bought and paid for. They expect, or at least hope, that there will be a reciprocal trade agreement: "I give you a present and you give me love," or "If you don't give me a present it means you don't love me." Then there is Cathy, who uses presents to hang on to relationships. She was so frightened of being abandoned as a child that she will now do anything to keep a friend. This year she went broke buying thirty-eight elaborate Christmas presents in an effort to ingratiate herself with people outside her own family because the ties within are so tenuous.

Mother's Day has particular significance and may be the most emotionally charged holiday for both alcoholics and their children. Alcohol information centers report that more calls come in on Mother's Day than on any other day of the year. "The phone rings off the hook," an alcoholism counselor says. "This may be because the family is feeling particularly deprived or sad when a mother is drunk or a father is absent and parents are not living up to anyone's expectations or fervent wishes." Again, the media, friends, and relatives are all part of a pressure group pushing toward a definition of "normal." And that means sober, functioning parents who are accessible and capable of giving and receiving. As the myth is perpetuated, the children of drinking parents are made to feel more guilt than usual. One man put it like this: "If I call my mother tomorrow, Mother's Day, she'll be drunk when she picks up the phone and she'll give me shit. But if I don't call, I'll feel guilty. Like which do you choose, guilt or shit?"

If you want to celebrate Mother's Day but your mother is still drinking, you may not feel much like honoring her with the kinds of syrupy sentiments the candy ads suggest. You may be more concerned with your own sadness or feelings of loss or anger. But there may have been a time when you had a marvelous, model mother and *she* may be the mother you will want to remember and celebrate. You might look at photographs from earlier years—of your mother as a girl or young woman. You might try talking to her sisters and brothers about how it used to be.

In some alcoholic families holidays are not so disrupted. One mother always pulled herself together for Christmas as she attempted to hide her problem from the relatives. A father managed to get himself to celebrations, but he was only there physically, not emotionally. As Dr. Steven J. Wolin of George Washington University has shown, in those families in which celebrations are kept intact, children are less likely to grow up to be alcoholic than in families in which rituals have been disrupted. Being able to do things as they have always been done lends stability to life.

In looking back on your own early life, you may be able to remember the times when everyone was together, and these celebrations may help explain why alcoholism did or did not find its way into your generation. If disruption rather than certainty was the norm, you may gain some understanding of why your parents behaved as they did. Not that this will erase the past, but it may make it easier to live with. Bill's father wasn't being mean and nasty when he sat on the gift record. He was blind to what it meant to his son. He didn't say to himself, "Here's Bill's *Nutcracker* record and I think I'll bust it up"—although it certainly looked that way.

One of the things about alcoholism that is hard to understand, particularly for a child, is that an act like breaking a record is not moral weakness or cussedness. It is the result of a disease that affects the brain in ways that may release violence or may deaden sensitivity to other people. Certainly indifference, unfulfilled promises, and destructive behavior are infuriating. But if your parent had a malignancy or another illness, anger would be an inappropriate response, and in some ways it is also an inappropriate response toward the alcoholic's behavior. Focused on past hurts or present disappointments, the anger can use up energy that might better be directed to recognizing what the present has to offer. There are ways to move out of these alcoholic entanglements. (See Chapter 11, "Getting Help.")

Dealing with Holiday Feelings

Some people feel that it is best to acknowledge that something has been lost and that it's okay to be sad. The mother of a six-month-old has finally come to accept the feeling that she was deprived of part of her childhood because her mother's heavy drinking made holidays into nightmares—and that her child will now be deprived of a grandmother's participation because she is still sick. She refuses to include her mother in her own family celebrations because she doesn't want to subject her baby to the vagaries of her mother's behavior. But she has a hard time resisting pressure from other family members, who are pushing her in not-so-subtle ways. "Mother is the weak one and you are the strong one. You should think of her and take care of her and invite her to share Christmas with you." Despite the guilt and sadness at excluding her mother and the fact that her family retaliates by ostracizing her, this woman is clear that her first priority is her own child, who at such a young age would not benefit by being exposed to the ups and downs of a drinking grandparent.

Clarifying priorities despite the feeling of not being a dutiful son or daughter is important. Some adult children of alcoholics feel guilty about not including their parents in their celebrations. Or they carry old, misplaced burdens because things are no better than they were in the past and they feel responsible for making improvements.

One woman committed herself to making things better for her present family. "When I was a kid Sundays were horrible—the pits. There was so much unstructured time. It seemed like straight downhill to Monday. My father was restless and my mother couldn't get it together to make any plans. She would go to church while we were delivered to Sunday school. When we got back home she would make an effort to make Sunday dinner, but it was always a flop; my father would be more interested in drinking than eating. I would drift in and out of his study as a way to keep in touch with him. But it didn't work; he drank more as the day wore on. I prayed for Monday to come. These days we plan things, and my ten-year-old pushes the planning. I guess he sees how uptight I get on weekends. He says we should *do* something, not just float around. So now I make a plan, but I try to keep it a flexible one. I recognize that we need a framework to have our family work together."

Some people have learned their lesson so well that they over-plan, down to the last picky detail of placecards for Thanksgiving dinner. That way, they feel, they can avoid the unpredictable incident that has wrecked so many other occasions.

Some people go to the other extreme. A sixth-grade teacher told her colleague, as they took their midmorning break, "With the holidays coming, I don't want to plan anything." It was as if the end of the world was imminent and she was preparing for it by abdicating responsibility and admitting her own helplessness in the face of it. Each year Halloween marked the beginning of classroom chaos and the start of the anxiety season. After it came Thanksgiving, Christmas, and the drinking event of the year— New Year's Eve. The fear that these drinking events stir up can be paralyzing.

One lawyer confesses, "Parties don't just remind me of what happened at home; they put me on the edge of my own drinking." Another man handles his anxiety by making a conscious decision not to let the holiday season throw him. He recalls what he sarcastically calls the "family triple-header": "Every year we would celebrate our parents' anniversary, my sister's birthday, and Thanksgiving all at once. It was a shambles and my poor sister would end up in tears; the others usually shrugged their shoulders and went their own way. This is absolutely not going to happen in my family." Now he limits his own entertaining to a manageable six people at a time and turns down any party when he knows ahead of time that drinking is to be the featured activity.

This may sound like a simplistic way of handling a difficult problem, but what this man really is doing is breaking the problem down into parts. The first step is to realize that he's drifted before. He doesn't have to keep doing what he has always done. Next, he has to realize that he can avoid big gatherings. He doesn't want to hurt anyone's feelings (that old fear of being abandoned if he doesn't do what others want him to do) but he has to learn to say no. "I felt stupid at first," he says, "but I practiced saying, 'Let's get together some other day when we can spend some time and talk.'" In time he worked out a suitable way to be with people that enabled him to feel much more at ease. What finally worked for him was the realization that he really could act like himself without being socially ostracized.

One woman who never saw New Year's Eve without a brawl when she was growing up now celebrates by going to church services in the evening. Another ignores the milestone and invites friends for brunch late the next morning. Instead of doing the thing you always did that never worked, do something completely different, as these people have done. You can keep the event low key and make it less of an emotional investment.

Avoid occasions that are automatically gala "eating and drinking" ones. Plan a boat ride, an evening at the movies, a stop for ice cream or pizza, a hike in the country, or a surprise visit. Start your own ways to make holidays fun. If celebrating with your family is too upsetting, go out with friends. As time goes on, families change and so do ways of doing things, even when alcohol has not been involved. A Thanksgiving at someone else's house instead of your own with your family may bring tears to your eyes. But as time goes on and you do it again, it will not be so strange or painful.

Disaster Planning

A family celebration often calls for continuing denial. "We knew and we didn't know" is how the child of an alcoholic puts it. "We didn't want to admit that our parents' drinking was any different from anyone else's." One way to forestall catastrophes is to have a family conference *before* the event. (This could easily be written into your family contract. See Chapter 8, "You and Your Parents Now.") Admit that drinking is a problem, even if the drinking person doesn't, and lay out clear groundrules. "If you come drunk we will all ask you to leave," for example. Or "If you drink here someone will be driving you home immediately." Then be sure at least one willing person is cautioned to keep an eye on things—to do the driving and to do the decision making if need be. Face reality and have other family members face reality too. Acknowledge the risks of leaving a young child alone with an active alcoholic, or driving with one, and recognize that self-preservation for you and the people you love is what really matters—even during holidays and special occasions! And if plans are drawn in conjunction with others, you won't feel so alone and responsible for the decisions that sometimes have to be made.

Finding New Allies

Look around for people who can help you through the holidays, particularly as you would like to celebrate them now. Al-Anon members may be the answer. (Al-Anon is for family and friends of the alcoholic. More about it in Chapter 11.) Talk to adult children from other alcoholic families who are relatively successful at handling their own difficulties. The support and understanding that come from others with similar concerns should not be underestimated. They can help fill the factual and emotional gaps that may have been left by a parent who was really not able to do the job.

Exploring New Role Models

"I never saw a party that didn't end in a fist fight," the son of an alcoholic explains when asked why he talks about inviting people over but never does anything about it. "If you never saw anyone read," he asks, "how could you know how to hold a book?" A young secretary, too, avoids inviting people because of her unbearable memories, and thereby perpetuates her loneliness. Celebrations in families where someone drinks too much are often so inappropriate that the memory of them still brings on rage and a rapid heartbeat. In one, the teenagers received canned screwdriver cocktails in their Christmas stockings. In another, presents weren't opened until Christmas night because the parents slept late after drinking the night before. The woman who says "I never had a sober role model" is determined that her daughter will grow up differently. Her new prototype is a neighbor who has developed family rituals she likes. "Now we get together in our living room every evening and talk over what happened during the day, as they do. That way 'togetherness' isn't something that happens once a year. When I was growing up," she recalls, "Christmas Eve was the time we had to suffer through the Dickens story. We never sat around as a family except for that one night a year. We had nothing to say to each other and we felt like strangers forced to spend the night together."

An eldest son who realized at eleven that his father was an alcoholic remembers, "Holidays were not a happy time. My family and grandparents got together and there was a lot of yelling, arguing, and screaming at one another. I remember going back to school totally exhausted and depressed."

You may have heard unending fighting and anger in your household too. But your present emotional state doesn't have to mirror the emotional context in which you grew up. The cast of characters is different, and you don't have to replay the same disaster scenes around the Thanksgiving turkey or the birthday candles. But that script may be so much a part of you that it will take conscious determination on your part to make changes. At first it may seem foolish and unnatural to adopt arbitrarily another family's ways, but as you change the awkwardness will disappear. Every party doesn't have to lead to an uproar; nor does every present have to be as inappropriate as the matched set of luggage one girl received when she was eight. Every New Year's Eve doesn't have to result in an array of bodies passed out on the floor and every Thanksgiving doesn't have to be the same as the last.

Pieces of old traditions can be combined with new ways. This will make your present-day celebrations less of an ordeal but still reminiscent of the good parts of bygone holidays. Now they will be more a reflection of the you of today than the you of yesterday—the you who then had little or no part in shaping any celebration.

PART II

Hangovers
from
Childhood

4

Who Are You Now?

I don't think you ever get over it—you just learn
to live with it.

Marsha, Age 41

Who is the *you* of today? And what makes you what you
are? Human beings are like snowflakes; no two are exactly alike. But since they were shaped by some of the
same forces, and family alcoholism is a powerful one, they share
certain characteristics. That's why you are likely to see yourself
reflected in the feelings and attitudes that other adult children of
alcoholics have identified as their own. Do you:

Lack trust?
Feel isolated and lonely?
Deny or suppress deep feelings?
Feel guilty?
Feel unnecessarily embarrassed and ashamed?
Wish for closeness, yet fear it?
Have a low opinion of yourself?
Feel sad?
Need to control yourself?
Need to control others?
Split the world into all good or all bad?
Have an exaggerated sense of responsibility?

Want desperately to please?
Have trouble standing up for your own needs?
Overreact to personal criticism?

If you answered yes several times and now have the feeling
that someone has been eavesdropping on your inner world, you
are not alone. Confronted with this list, many children of alcoholics say, "That's me, all right. How did you know?"

The Classic Roles

It's not hard to know. These personality traits develop early
and are part of the pattern of survival that helps children in alcoholic families adjust, no matter how unstable or difficult their lives
may be. These children also assume certain identifiable roles that
enable them, to one degree or another, not only to grow up successfully but to *seem* as healthy as anyone else, at least for a while.
These roles have been skillfully detailed by Sharon Wegscheider
in her book *Another Chance: Hope and Health for the Alcoholic
Family.*

The Family Hero, she says, is the child on whom the family
counts to take over when others flounder. He or she is successful
both at home and at school, does everything right, and wins a
place by receiving praise for taking care of others, actually becoming a "junior mom." At school he helps the teacher, is a leader
among his peers, and does well scholastically and often athletically
too. He is looked upon for leadership by other children and
praised by adults.

As an adult he often goes into the helping professions, for those
roles are both familiar and satisfying to him. He does well no matter what career choice he makes and often rises rapidly. Ultimately he pays a price, for he has trouble feeling good about
himself no matter how successful he becomes. He feels guilty
much of the time, and since he is so accustomed to running things
he is ill at ease, even frightened, when not in control. As he attempts to control those around him, he becomes a workaholic.
This striving for success takes a physical toll, which may result in
physiological, stress-related problems such as heart attacks and
strokes. Those of his children who emulate him and fail are prone
to alcoholism.

Next is the Scapegoat, who is often the second child and is nearly always involved in some kind of unsanctioned behavior or naughtiness, leading to his identification in the family as the troublemaker or misfit. It is within that role that he gets the attention he needs, and he continues to raise Cain as he is blamed for all family mishaps. He feels hurt, angry, and abandoned. He begins early in life running around with gangs of young people, is often a truant, and gets into trouble with drugs and alcohol. As a teenager, the Scapegoat runs up against the law and may be arrested for drunk driving. He pays the highest price because he may end up in jail and is the child most likely to kill himself, either accidentally or on purpose.

The Lost Child or Quiet One, often referred to as "the angel," is always in the background and never causes trouble. He spends a great deal of time in his own room away from the family, has no opinions, and feels hopeless and unimportant. He retreats into himself, is sad, confused, and fearful. In school he never speaks up, has no opinions, and is easily lost in the shuffle. The personal price he pays is immense, for his personality is flat and joyless. He does not learn to do well but gets attention by becoming sick with ailments such as asthma and allergies. Ultimately he has sexual identity problems and often marries several times or not at all. He may become an overeater, using food to comfort himself and make up for the emptiness within.

The last coping role is the Mascot, who is tense, anxious, and often overactive. He is the one who defuses explosive situations by focusing attention on himself. He will do a somersault in the middle of a therapy session in order to distract everyone, and he manages, through humor, to ease tense moments. He clowns incessantly and eventually uses tranquilizers to calm himself down. Because he is a silly adult, his relationships are shallow and flighty. Psychiatric illnesses and suicide are ways he uses to get out of it all.

You will undoubtedly see yourself in one, and possibly more, of these descriptions. Wegscheider points out that children (and adults) who once clung to a particular coping role can and do change to others, depending on what's most expedient at a given time.

In one family someone had to take on the mundane chores of everyday living when the eldest son and Family Hero went off to college. In this case, the Mascot, although only twelve years old and seemingly immature for his age, jumped into the caretaking role. He learned how to do simple cooking and cleaning up and even managed to relay phone calls responsibly to his working mother. He quickly became the new Family Hero.

The roles most often interchanged are the Hero and the Scapegoat. For example, when the Scapegoat gets better through treatment, he may begin to improve at school or begin to help around the house. Then, when family approval focuses on him, the Hero will become upset and take his place by using drugs or behaving obstreperously in order to keep his spot in the limelight.

These descriptions are not intended to be rigid scenarios. They are guides to enable you to understand why you behave in different ways at different times. The coping roles and "typical" characteristics described can steer you onto the track of some of the problems you may still be having and give you a good clue as to how they began, but you shouldn't try too hard to fit yourself into a pigeonhole.

Human nature is so complex and psychological makeup so infinitely complicated and difficult to understand that it would be hazardous to say flatly, "Adult children of alcoholics are this way or that way." In trying to say categorically that children of alcoholics behave in certain ways we do not take into account how children who do not have alcoholic parents behave and the ways they may be no different. Owen, a forty-five-year-old homeowner, has been trying to finish building a dining room table for three years and has never been able to get himself to complete it. He says he never finishes what he starts and often gets bogged down in minutiae. A friend assumed that Owen had an alcoholic parent because he had read that children of alcoholics seem to be unable to finish tasks. He had fallen into a trap; Owen had no alcoholism in his family. We cannot say that *all* human beings of any particular kind behave in any one way. Assuming that because a person is part of a group he or she necessarily takes on all the characteristics of that group is simplistic thinking. Nor can we be sure that a person with certain traits must belong to a given group. Even though most schizophrenics act erratically, not all people who act erratically are schizophrenic. As for adult children of alcoholics, their responses to their home situations vary, just as their personalities do. But it is often more possible in these cases than in others to trace a coping strategy back to what was behind it—the misuse of alcohol in the family.

Inability to Trust

Coming from a family where there is too much drinking means you can't be sure of others even when they are reliable. How in the world can you trust when there has never been anyone in your life you could count on? You may be so crippled by this inability to trust that even when someone says something nice, you don't believe it. The automatic response to "I like you" is apt to be "Why?" or "Prove it!" The skepticism is always there. One man put it simply: "I can't let people I'm with know me or get really close. I never share my innermost thoughts with people because I just can't be sure."

Let's look at two distinct, but related, kinds of trust. One is trusting others; the other is trusting yourself. Children of alcoholics have learned that they can't count on the alcoholic, and therefore they are fearful. "If I trust you, you will take over and control me. I can't risk it." No wonder it is difficult to become involved in long-term commitments or marriages. Even passing friendships, daily encounters with fellow workers, and casual meetings give rise to an element of standoffishness.

People who trust others seem to be able to identify trustworthy people. Asked about their method, they say, "Well, you just feel it in your bones." "I trust a certain friend because he is not trying to make me think anything special about him; he has no ax to grind, and he isn't trying to get anything from me." "I go on how people feel about me—their interest in me and my experience with them in the past. I ask myself, 'Have they done what they've said they were going to do?' I expect people to do the nice or right thing but I'm not shocked when they don't."

Children of alcoholics have different expectations. A child who learns early that no one can be counted on learns equally early to depend on himself or herself, and to be fiercely protective of this autonomy. To the outside world, it may look like precious, praiseworthy independence; but to the inner child who craves care, it is a high price to pay for survival. When you cannot allow yourself

to believe in other people, there is a reflexive pulling back in order
to make yourself feel safe. But that withdrawal also intensifies
feelings of being alone.

When someone reacts to what seems like your aloofness with
the unspoken attitude of "I don't want to be close to you," you
may immediately feel, "I don't need you anyway." Perhaps that's
what you have said inside your own head to your alcoholic parent.
You may find yourself going through life warding off potential
hurts. "I told Jim to get out before he could say he was thinking
about it. It's safest to be alone."

Another way of reacting to inner emptiness is to put up a good
front, keep busy, have many friends, and smile frantically all the
time. At college, one young son of an alcoholic mother "felt totally
alone even though I was popular. I knew a lot of people, but nobody knew me." The opposite side of the coin is the inability to
trust yourself, despite what looks like independence. "I'm never
sure that what I think is right, even about a TV show. I wait to
hear what other people say," an intelligent twenty-eight-year-old
New Yorker says. Her perceptions were so often challenged when
she was young ("I never said that . . .") that now she can't decide
about anything. She distrusts her feelings too. She has pretended
that everything was all right for so long that she "can't tell if I'm
really sad or really angry, or if I'm faking it." Another woman says,
"I've never seen my parents cry and I never cry either. You feel
too vulnerable when you cry. I got very good at the superficial
stuff. I laugh a lot. I didn't know until recently what a real emotion was."

Sometimes the difference between laughing to release tension
and laughing to hide a deeper emotion you are afraid to express is
hard to recognize. If your laughing borders on crying you can suspect that you are covering up painful feelings. One woman in
group therapy laughs each time she talks about the antics of her
alcoholic mother. She describes how she treated her four children
like baby chicks, scattering popcorn on the floor for them to pick
up in their "beaks." When she talks about her mother she laughs,
but she soon cries.

Another woman in group therapy laughs and cries whenever
she talks about herself. In her particular family, expressing unhap-
piness or dissatisfaction was unacceptable. Since it was not to be
openly expressed, it was disguised. She learned to conceal her true

feelings by laughing when she talked about anything that was important to her. After a while, the laughing became a habit and a smile came across her face each time she felt something deeply— not because there was anything funny, but because she felt she shouldn't show negative emotions. Her mother's drinking had resulted in constant high glee and hilarity, which also served to cover over the sad reality.

The son of an alcoholic man laughs each time he expresses a serious thought. Because of self-doubt, he has developed a veneer that makes light of his own feelings. Since he is never quite sure whether or not what he says is going to be valued (he was never taken seriously by his alcoholic father), he escapes the risk of ridicule by making light of any straightforward thought he may have. Also, having been so constantly slapped down, he is afraid of being wrong and doesn't trust himself enough to have the courage of his convictions. In laughing at himself he can transform a positive statement into a joke or banter and deftly change important matters into insignificant ones.

Laughing at yourself or at others can be a creative way to cope and at times can serve a purpose. But when it obscures the problem, you have to search for another way of getting at what is really wrong.

Anger and Other Time Bombs

Laughter is not helpful when it consistently covers up deep feelings that are so buried you are hardly aware of the force they build up inside you. One of these powerful feelings is anger. You may have been told not to be angry in the same way that you were told to control your other emotional reactions. Or perhaps, to this day, you haven't been able to recognize or feel the anger. But if it is not acknowledged, it seethes under the surface, erupting at unexpected times; and when it is pushed under again you live with a constant sense of dissatisfaction, a sense of missing something, a sense of having been gypped or left out. As the anger festers but continues to be ignored, it may literally eat away at the innards, leading to somatic illnesses such as ulcers and hypertension.

Most adult children of alcoholics live with anger that began as a result of the contradictions built into life with a parent whose personality and demands changed abruptly with changes in blood alcohol level. A woman says, "I had two mothers. I could never put them together into one person." Another recalls her father: "When he was sober he called me an angel. When he was drunk he called me a whore."

Children learn to accommodate, but they live with a slow fuse that's burning. "One day mother wants the towels folded in three, the next time she wants them folded in two. What do you do?" One thing children do is become very wary, watching for warning signals. Some become quiet. "I learned to tiptoe and never to have an opinion," the daughter of an alcoholic father remembers. Recognizing that it is the alcohol that caused (or causes) the unexplained shifts is helpful: "If I understand that her thinking is the result of the drinking, I'm less angry and mixed up. I now know her ambiguity is a symptom of the problem. For a long time I couldn't give a name to what was happening; I didn't understand that the peculiar behavior was related to the drinking. I knew something was screwy, but I didn't know what or why. When I saw how other people acted, I felt as if she wasn't part of the same human race. I still have feelings of my own that I don't have a label for."

Others have concurred. When they finally were able to identify the problem, it became more understandable and thus less frightening. It is as if giving something a name gives you power over it. This is the message of the famous German fairy tale "Rumpelstiltskin."

Another story, probably apocryphal, sums up both the unpredictability and the irrationality of the alcoholic. A man asked his wife to make him two eggs for breakfast, one fried and one scrambled. She shrugged her shoulders but dished up the eggs, prepared according to order. As she put them in front of him he yelled, "I can't eat these. You scrambled the one I wanted fried, and fried the one I wanted scrambled."

Unpredictability of this kind causes everything from aggravation to fury. Not surprisingly, some people use this anger to serve their own purposes. A fifty-year-old woman says, "I feel comfortable with anger. I use it like a weapon to keep people away. For me, it's safer to be angry than to let people get close."

Beverly Nichols, the author of fifty books, wrote in his autobiography, *Father Figure*, that he was so angry he actually tried to kill his father, a retired lawyer who was an alcoholic. When he was fifteen, he slipped crushed aspirin into his father's soup. When that failed, he ran a heavy roller over his father as he napped on the lawn. A third time, he gave him a heavy dose of sleeping pills and abandoned him in the snow. (Nothing hidden here!) His father perversely survived.

Guilt

If Beverly Nichols didn't feel guilty after these attempted murders, he was a rare person. The ability to feel guilt makes human beings human. If we didn't all experience it in some form, the ways we relate to one another and think about ourselves would be entirely different. Guilt is a uniquely human emotion, aroused by behavior contrary to social commandment, and we all know how uncomfortable it can be. We try to explain it in order to get rid of it and go so far as to endow our pets with it: "My dog felt guilty when he chewed up the pot holder. He lowered his chin and looked up at me with those soulful eyes."

Great writers and philosophers have tussled with the concept. Shakespeare used it to explain the behavior of many of his characters, the Bible tries to interpret it, religions rely on it to keep people on the "straight and narrow," and parents use it to control their children. Freud built theory on it. He wrote that the basis of the sense of guilt is the unconscious and, in men, is related to a wish to possess their mother and get rid of their father. For men and women, hostility and aggressive impulses that are quelled are transformed into guilt.

As far as treating alcoholism goes, guilt has been called a useless emotion. Nevertheless, it exists and there are times when behavior justifies it. Then we take the consequences or settle for living with the resulting rotten feelings. For example, family members usually have a profound sense of failure that gives rise to guilt, generated by the inability to rescue the alcoholic or make the family different.

People who report that they have often wondered what would happen if their parents died have lingering guilt, even though, according to psychologists, most people wish, consciously or unconsciously, at one time or another, that a parent would die. Sometimes that wish stems from the sexual relationship between parents: a girl wishes her mother to die so she can have her father;

a boy would like to get rid of his father in order to have his mother to himself. For the adult child of an alcoholic, that wish has particular significance because the alcoholic is often so sick that the possibility of having it come true is real. If it does come true, the child is convinced that he or she caused the parent to die.

A young author said that he wished his alcoholic parents would evaporate or go up in smoke. He blamed himself, not them, for what had gone on. He still searches for a way to absolve himself from the guilt originating in the persistent death fantasies. (His parents are alive and his father is still drinking heavily.) Inappropriate role reversals are often linked to this wish, making real what is only a fantasy in most children's lives. If a father is drinking, a son may take over for him, fixing things around the house, watching over the younger children, listening to family troubles, and even giving advice. He may act like "the man of the house," but there is lasting guilt at having replaced or "killed off" the alcoholic.

Embarrassment and Shame

Embarrassment may have fewer emotional consequences than guilt, but it is extremely uncomfortable nevertheless. Most people have experienced their own parents as an embarrassment. Their clothes were either too expensive or too plain, their voices too soft or too gruff. They paid too much attention to their children's friends or not enough. For the children of alcoholics, the embarrassment is multiplied to painful proportions.

"What will the neighbors think?" is always an overwhelming concern. Supposing someone pops in unannounced and sees or hears what's really going on? Sometimes the neighbors know very little. At other times the results of the drinking are flamboyantly obvious. A suburban man announced his drunkenness when, as his son puts it: "He neglected to open the garage door before inserting the car."

The day Anna's family was set to move, her father began drinking early in the morning. By the time the movers arrived, he was dead drunk. Unfazed, they lifted him up along with the furniture and propped him up in the open truck in his own chair. Then they drove two miles to the new apartment. Anna says she didn't think about her father's welfare during the bumpy trip; she worried only about whether the new neighbors would see him "being moved."

"My mother used to pick me up from school dressed in her raincoat with her nightgown hanging out below it. She would flirt with my friends," says the son of an alcoholic. "I wanted to die." Still another would cross the street any time he saw his mother coming toward him unsteadily. The shame is so intense because the stigma attached to drunkenness is so powerful.

And because of the stigma, it is difficult to help children (and adults) get those deep-down secret shames to surface.

A thirty-four-year-old social worker in group therapy with others who grew up with alcoholism said her shame was so overwhelming she had never before talked about her father's "problem," even to her former therapist, whom she had seen over a period of three years. It was easier to talk about her homosexuality than to mention the drinking.

An experienced elementary schoolteacher has learned to open the door to class discussions of uncomfortable topics by saying, "All families have problems. Sometimes there is no daddy at home, sometimes there is a very sick person to take care of, sometimes there is a new baby in the family, and sometimes there is someone who drinks too much." This approach neutralizes the stigma of alcoholism and puts it on a par with other family difficulties. A child can then feel freer to volunteer that drinking is the problem in the family just as another child might say, with the same amount of feeling, that his father needs new shoes and there isn't enough money to buy another pair. At the finish of a discussion of family problems, one little girl could bring herself to divulge her shameful secret only by writing in the palm of her hand, "My mom is alcoholic." Then she opened her hand to reveal the message to her astounded teacher.

The effects of this kind of embarrassment last. "I can't listen to Beatles records," said one disc jockey. "I put them on and take off the earphones. When I was a kid my friends and I played those records all day. My drunk father would come hurtling into the basement where we played, yelling at all of us, 'Turn that stuff off. Get out of this house. What kind of a place do you think this is?' I felt like dying inside. Finally I didn't have friends over any more. It wasn't worth it. The embarrassment was too much."

The old embarrassment keeps adult children of alcoholics on

the lookout for awkward social situations. They need to be extra
cautious when strangers are about. They try hard to do the right
thing at the right time and to learn what is expected of them and
of those who "belong" to them. They make an extra effort to wear
appropriate clothing, use the proper utensils, say the right thing.
Their behavior has to be fitting, their speech has to be correct.
They would rather not meet friends than risk another embarrassing scene.

Some feel what they characterize as "generalized embarrassment," a kind of perpetual stage fright. They feel it when they arrive at a meeting and other participants are already seated. They
have a constant sense of personal exposure. They say that sometimes they blush spontaneously when there isn't anything to blush
about. Awkward feelings come flooding back. Sometimes they are
cued by present-day circumstances that revive early scenes, and
sometimes they seem to come out of nowhere.

Whatever the early embarrassing reality has been, most people
want their families to be perfect or, at least, as good as anyone
else's. Let someone outside the family say, "Your father is a
drunk," and the ranks quickly close. Loyalty to loved ones is a
basic tenet of family life. One therapist evoked these fiercely protective feelings when he joined his fourteen-year-old client in the
tirades against his parents. When the therapist said, "Yes, your dad
really sounds like a bastard," the boy came back with a barrage of
positives about his father and reported that he felt like beating the
therapist up.

This kind of fierce loyalty may have kept you and others like
you from getting help. "When my teacher asked me if there was
any trouble at home, I said no, even though I knew I couldn't keep
my mind on my work because my mom and dad had argued all
night and kept me up. But I wasn't going to tell *her*." This is a
common response to attempts to help. A man who spent six years
in an institution for neglected children because his father was
drinking heavily and couldn't take care of the family still got into
fights when he finally returned home and overheard nasty remarks
about his father who was "lying in the gutter for everyone to see."

If you still feel ashamed or embarrassed, remember you are not
your father or your mother. What they do and say does not reflect
on you or change in any way who you are today.

When young people are ashamed of their parents every day,

the shame can spread to a feeling of being ashamed of themselves. Even though it often goes unrecognized or unacknowledged, shame may be *the* most powerful emotion for adult children of alcoholics. Guilt can be ameliorated and embarrassment can be minimized or eradicated, but shame goes on as self-hatred, which renders the individual unable to form constant close relationships. If you see yourself as "untouchable," "dirty," or "less than human," you naturally stay apart and away from others. Closeness is out of the question and intimacy impossible.

While many parents accuse their children of causing the alcoholism, and the children believe what they say, some go on to demoralize their children in other ways. "Get off my lap, you smell." "I can't stand looking at your dirty hair." "You're a pig, don't get near me." At the same time, the parent does nothing to teach ordinary physical cleanliness and general hygiene. No one teaches the child to bathe, to brush hair, to cut nails, or to brush teeth. One man remembers lice in his hair and long dirty toenails. A woman says she feels "dirty inside" and is ashamed in front of her husband when she is menstruating.

Shame generated by neglectful parents is devastating to the child at any age because the child subscribes to the parents' attitudes. And that devastation lasts and is internalized. It leads to feelings of low self-esteem and depression of a special kind.

Sadness and Mourning

Dr. Susan Deakins, attending psychiatrist at Washington Heights Community Service Center in New York, notes that adult children of alcoholics who are depressed have a lingering sadness that underlies their depression. She says this sadness and sudden, unexpected outbursts of tears can appear at any time, triggered in reaction to kindness. "It happens when people act in a caring manner toward children of alcoholics, a manner never shown by their parents," she says. "This brings the realization that one's parents should have offered more emotionally than they did and leads to mourning a relationship that never was."

This reaction also surfaces in remembering a good parent who began the destructive drinking when, say, the child was in his or her teens, and the drinking became more serious over the years. As adults, these "children" remember a wonderful parent from when they were young. And they mourn the loss of that parent. Joanie remembers when her mother took loving care of her family, worked, and was a "super mom." Twenty years later Joanie has a family of her own, but her mother can't function well enough to understand that she is missing the fun she could be having with her own grandchildren. She is drunk most of the time. And Joanie continues to wish for the good mother she once had.

There are times when sadness is compounded by guilt. It is not quite acceptable in our society to mourn the living; it is not even understandable to most people. Joanie doesn't have the social support she would have if her mother had died—no friends and relatives joining her in her grief, writing comforting condolence letters. Even though her feeling of loss is real and appropriate, she is nevertheless critical of herself for her reactions.

Control

Some of the sadness that envelops adult children like a cloud is related to a sense of having little grasp or control over their own destiny. Since they are often helpless, they feel hopeless or out of control. There are three kinds of control involved: the control other people have over them; the control they have over other people and events; and the control they exert over their own bodies and minds. At times these all seem to blend into one overall sense of lack of mastery.

As is true in so many homes where someone is drinking too much, controls are invisible or nonexistent and children may ask themselves: "Am I in control? Who is in control? Is anyone in control here?" When no one is in charge, there can be a frightening kind of freedom that is a burden as well as a gift.

One woman couldn't understand why no one set rules for her or told her what to do and when to do it; she felt neglected rather than free. It seemed to her that no one cared and she was in constant danger. In contrast, another woman said that one of the best things about her childhood was the wonderful amount of freedom she and her brother had. They could come and go whenever they wanted; they never had to let anyone know where they were; and they were never told not to go to other people's homes for meals or the night. "No one told me not to ride on my boyfriend's motorbike, not to wear high heels to school, not to stay out late, not to skip breakfast. My friends had to go home to their homework and chores. They had a million restrictions. I had none and I loved it."

But lack of control can be frightening. Because of their experience with a drinking parent, some adult children feel they have to keep the lid on tightly to keep their bad selves from emerging. Total self-control is idealized; it is the antithesis of alcoholism. The conviction that only absolute power is worthwhile slips over into other areas of life so that if control eludes them they feel defeated. These children always drive the car, plan the meals, choose vacation spots, and arrange the furniture. They must do all this or they feel like victims and see themselves as having no say in their lives. Everything is done to them. This too is understandable. One woman identified this attitude of helplessness as a familiar technique she uses to manipulate others, and then added, "But I really was a victim. At three months my mother burned me with a cigarette."

In order to make themselves more comfortable, some adult children feign control, put up a good front, and pretend that everything's fine even when it isn't. This tactic is learned at home where the person who was drinking was a constant preoccupation for all family members—especially for the alcoholic, who was always attempting to control the drinking and denying that he or she couldn't. The lesson is so well learned by repetition, if no other way, that the child continues to strive for control and feels right only when he or she has it.

Timmen L. Cermak, M.D., and Stephanie Brown, Ph.D., organizers of the National Association of Children of Alcoholics, point out that in such children "intense feelings of depression, loss, and joy are all experienced primarily as a feeling of being out of control and are accompanied by feelings of anxiety, panic, and vulnerability. More important and frightening than the actual emotion is the sense of lack of control."

Bringing up a child can intensify this sense of panic. It is, after all, in the nature of children to defy control. Christie has a two-year-old who throws food off the high chair and won't go to sleep when her parents are tired and ready for the day to be over. Christie becomes distraught. One day she hit the child because she spit food onto the clean kitchen floor. Then she was terrified that she would become the child abuser her mother had been. Her reaction was impulsive. She had done something that, when rational, she certainly would not have considered. It is the loss of control over her own actions and better judgment that terrifies her.

There is a flip side to problems of control that has to do with making changes. If everything has to be carefully planned and just as carefully carried out, with no deviation possible without panic, how can anything be made different? Then too, accustomed to being rigid or immobilized as they tried to keep the peace at home, how can grownup children of alcoholics trust themselves to try anything new? They feel like victims rather than active partic- ipants in deciding their own fate.

Sometimes they react to the feeling of victimization with the sense that having control is surviving. "I must have control; I watch the clock; I always know everything that's happening. There's a positive part to that too, because I can tune into people's needs, but at the same time it takes away from the spontaneity I might have." Like many other adult children, Pamela, a sales- woman, is distressed by her lack of mastery over her environment, and she is ill at ease when there are outside forces that she feels are at work determining her future. She becomes noticeably agitated when she doesn't know exactly what's around the corner or how she can make things turn out the way she wants them. Even a fallen omelette will set her back. But particularly disturbing is the loss of control over her own body. Lack of physical coordination when she can't catch a thrown ball or thread a needle dismays her more than the situation calls for.

Whatever the kind of control involved, the concern with it is easy to trace to childhood in the alcoholic household where things may have been literally beyond control. You didn't know if you would be praised for clearing the table or smacked because you did it too soon. When you stayed away from the house for the af- ternoon, you didn't know if you would be punished for being away so long or if no one would even notice. Most unnerving of all, you had no power to make the difference. The world seemed threaten- ing and unpredictable.

Splitting the World

An alcoholic parent is often kind and loving when sober but has a very different, hurtful personality when drunk or hung over.

"At work even now," says a computer operator, "I see people as either bullies who will beat me up or as friends who absolutely love me." This tendency to see the world and the people in it in fairy-tale fashion as all good or all bad, is common for children of alcoholic parents. After all, that's the way it seemed.

It's important as an adult to recognize that this view of people doesn't make sense. If someone hurts you, that person should not necessarily become all evil. If someone helps, that person does not automatically become a saint. People are infinitely more complex. One son of an alcoholic father recalled, "When I was a child it either rained or it didn't. There were no in-betweens. Now, there are a lot of gray days."

Most children stop splitting people or events into good or bad as a natural part of growing up. The fairy princess and the evil witch are both put into perspective. Childhood fantasies and wishes are left behind and the real world takes over. Gray days may be sad, but not intolerable. And they are closer to reality than unadulterated sunshine or constant storms.

And Now—The Aftereffects

With all these blows to the inner self and such a distorted view of reality, it is no wonder that children of alcoholism feel unworthy of the kind of recognition and respect most people take for granted. The hangovers from childhood continue to affect daily living even after the alcoholic family has gone the way of all nuclear families—spread out and aged. In your own home now you may find yourself unable to accept help from your children or your spouse—you can do it yourself, thank you. But the truth is you may feel you don't deserve that kind of ordinary consideration. Outside the immediate family, many problems that commonly beset adult children of alcoholics are intensified or brought into focus when they are planning a career or actually holding down a job.

The confusion begins as soon as career goals are to be set. The adult child of an alcoholic is often convinced from the very beginning that if a career is chosen, he or she won't be able to carry it out. Then, once the job begins, the fears multiply. Here are the old messages rising to the top again: You're incompetent; you don't count; you can't make a difference. These negative images, which often get in the way of friendships and family closeness, are magnified at work.

However, there are ways in which children of alcoholism make very *good* employees:

- They are out to please and therefore don't question authority (even though their anger and frustration may make the quality of their work lower than it would be otherwise).

- They see the workplace as a safe environment where they can be cared for. (A mechanic said, "At work I feel real; at home my wife doesn't understand me.")

- They keep people at a distance and therefore concentrate on work to be done rather than taking time off or using it to become involved with other employees.

- They have an exaggerated sense of responsibility (particularly true of Super Copers).

- They are used to handling stress and functioning well under pressure.

And there are ways in which adult children make very *poor* employees:

- They are so afraid of success they don't do their best, or undermine their own efforts.

- They become emotionally out of control, particularly when feeling pushed around, unappreciated, or overlooked. (They missed so much that they envy people who get ahead.)

- They equate salary with appreciation and/or love. They avoid asking for a deserved raise and then are resentful because they feel exploited.

- They are oversensitive if their performance is questioned and traumatized if criticized. Therefore, they don't ask for help and would rather make errors than ask how something should be done.

- They are confused about independence and dependence. They want to be relied upon and at the same time to lean on others.

(This particular characteristic often leads to conflicts with authority.)

- They doubt their own ability and therefore accept jobs that do not require their full potential; then they become bored but blame themselves for not being satisfied.

- They feel they try hard, but are never good enough.

This was certainly true of a forty-year-old woman (a recovering alcoholic) who wanted to walk out on a good job because she didn't think she could keep up the required pace. "In my head I have a tape," she said. "It's my alcoholic father's voice telling me, 'You'll never do it right.' " Her company's alcoholism counselor suggested to her that she replace that tape with one of her own or with her mother's encouraging voice and message: "You don't have to listen to the old tape any more." Now she says the tapes play at the same time, but the positive one is louder.

Of course, these characterizations of the adult children of alcoholics are generalizations. If taken too literally, they can be upsetting, particularly if you try to fit yourself into the picture exactly in accordance with what you have read. The descriptions are meant only as guides to aspects of your own personality that you might want to watch for. Your behavior in any specific situation— at work, at school, with friends, on vacation—could be a reflection, a mirror image, of the way in which you deal with other aspects of your life. And as you hold up that mirror, you may look into it closely enough to see what you have never seen so clearly before.

5

You and
Your Drinking

What is your favorite obsession?
All obsessions are favorites.

Ann, Age 28

Y ou may be tempted to ignore your own drinking, but as the child of an alcoholic you need to pay special attention to your use of any drug. Many people from alcoholic homes find themselves caught up in some form of addictive behavior—drinking, taking pills, smoking, overeating, overworking, gambling. Yet alcoholic beverages exert a peculiar fascination and carry a strong emotional charge. Children of alcoholism of any age always have a very special feeling about drinking—their own and others'. It is most often a push-pull situation full of conflicting attitudes, beliefs, and behaviors. Either they drink too much or they abstain. Or they may try to find a middle ground after a long struggle. In the meantime the experimenting, ambivalence, and confusion continue.

Sometimes the conflict is unconscious and is noticeable only to an outsider. At a dinner party one night a group of friends engaged in unending talk about where the wine had come from, whether or not it was suitable and cold enough, how much it had cost, how interesting the shape of the bottle was, and on and on. Then the hostess went through an agonizing choice, the upshot of which was that she would not allow herself a taste of the wine. Still, she insisted on keeping her friends' glasses filled and continued to pour wine long after they said they had had plenty. All during dinner it was impossible to carry on a coherent conversation about anything else. Much of the time the hostess held a half-empty bottle of wine in her left hand while she ate with her right. She never actually drank any, but the topic was never entirely dropped.

The hostess had grown up with an erratic alcoholic father and had never been able to achieve a neutral attitude toward liquor. She had believed she could control her father's drinking by doing "the right thing," which translated into holding the bottle, or keeping it away from him.

You don't have to look hard to discover that extreme reactions to alcohol have their roots in childhood. Many children in alcoholic homes equate *a drink* with *a drunk.* They almost never see social drinking so they become extremely edgy when there is any drinking. Some, in fact, are more familiar with abstinence, which they have seen in a recovering parent or grandparent, than they are with ordinary social drinking. As these children grow up, they have to learn that it is possible to drink without getting drunk.

Many of these adults feel attraction rather than aversion to liquor. After all, for some people, alcohol seems to perform wonders. After even a single drink they are able to take a carefree part in social situations. Alcohol does, in fact, tend to loosen the tongue and give people a sense of well-being, easy sociability, even elation, which can seem enviable to the child of an alcoholic. For these supposedly cheerful drinkers, alcohol takes away immediate troubles and takes "the monkey" off their backs (although it may later put a heavier one on). They feel more able to try things that they would ordinarily find terrifying. Alcohol can appear to be a wonder drug until the moment of truth—the moment it traps you.

Since the response to alcohol is likely to be genetically determined, you as the child of an alcoholic must be particularly wary of the temptations of social ease, of trying to overcome feelings of shyness or embarrassment through alcohol. Once you begin to solve psychological stress by drinking, the stage is set for trouble. It would be good if a reliable predictor could be found to identify who will become alcoholic before abnormal drinking begins. Then what often seems to be inevitable might become avoidable. Much recent research has focused on "biological markers"—signals indicating a person's susceptibility. (See Chapter 9, "How Did It Happen?")

At the same time, sociologists and psychologists are looking into the question. In a twenty-year longitudinal study by Dorothy Miller and Michael Jang of the Institute for Scientific Analysis, children of alcoholics were compared with children of nonalcoholics on five points having to do with the *percentage* of "Subjects Agreement with Items on Personal Effects of Alcohol." If some of these items catch your attention, you may want to use the accompanying table to check yourself.

Effect of Alcohol	Children of Alcoholics (%)	Children of Nonalcoholics (%)
Helps me forget I am not the kind of person I really want to be.	11	3
Helps me get along better with other people.	16	8
Helps me feel more satisfied with myself.	8	4
Helps me forget my problems.	15	13
Helps give me confidence in myself.	12	9

As the table suggests, children of alcoholics expect more from alcohol than children of nonalcoholics.

How to Say No

The role of an abstainer in our "liquid" society is not an easy one. Unless you are part of a community that for religious or other reasons avoids alcohol, you will be faced continually with situations in which you have to make a choice.

When you say no to a drink, particularly when other people are drinking and it is the expected thing to do, you automatically call attention to yourself and to the fact that you are not drinking. Any feelings you may already have of being different will be reinforced. You may worry that others will see you as a religious nut, a prude, a party pooper, or, worst of all, an alcoholic. Although the social dictates about drinking are changing, you may still overhear a snicker or a crude remark about people who don't drink. Any of these could lead to weakening your resolve.

How are you going to say no and feel good about it? First of all, you have a right not to drink just as you have a right to have or not have a child, to speak your mind in the media or in public places, to subscribe to the religion you prefer or to no religion at all. Only when the lives or property of others are jeopardized should you be subjected to sanctions. If you know you have a right to your choice, then the power of conviction behind that choice will be apparent and appreciated by others; and they will be more reluctant to challenge you.

There are hundreds of ways of saying no. The one you choose will depend on your personal preference or style. "No, thank you" is one that is simple, tried, and true. Or, just as good, "I've had enough, thank you." "Do you have anything nonalcoholic?" "I'm not drinking tonight." "I've given up drinking." If you feel uncomfortable at being blunt, perhaps you should invent and stick to a graceful lie. "No, thanks, doctor's orders." You may want to accept the drink if there is a particularly insistent host or hostess. It's easy to hold a glass. You can then pour the drink down the drain or out the window later. For some peculiar reason, people who are drinking don't care if you're not drinking as long as they see you holding a glass with liquid in it. A nonalcoholic beverage will do the trick as well as an alcoholic one. The point is, you don't have to drink if you don't want to.

The Alcohol Checkup

How can you monitor your drinking to find out if you are handling it well or poorly? At times this is extremely hard for people from alcoholic homes. Many are worried about losing control once they've begun to drink. Even if they enjoy drinking, they may not know how to take control directly and have periodically experienced the uncomfortable and frightening feelings that go along with loss of control. If you have never lived with normal drinking, you may have no standard against which to measure your own drinking. By using the CAGE test (an acronym of the key words), developed by Dr. John Ewing of the University of North Carolina, you can begin to assess your own drinking:

1. Have you felt the need to   Cut down on your drinking?

2. Have you ever felt   Annoyed by criticism of
your drinking?

3. Have you had   Guilt feelings about drinking?

4. Do you ever take a morning   Eye-opener?

Of course, no cut-and-dried questions and answers can tell you definitely whether you are developing a drinking problem. The most they can do is alert you to what you are doing. Keeping a drinking diary is one way to watch. Write down, for a week, with scrupulous honesty when, where, and with whom you drink. Another way, which is simple and reasonable, is to measure your drinks by using a jigger (one and a half ounces). How much alcohol are you really swallowing? If you feel you are drinking too much, you will have some indication of what triggers it and where it takes place. Then you may want to consider making some changes.

There are other ways and other tests to help you identify early signs of alcoholism. Here are some questions randomly selected from a variety of quizzes:

- Are you beginning to lie or feel guilty about your drinking?

- Do you turn to alcohol to make yourself feel better?

- Do you make excuses for the reasons you drink?

- Do you gulp your drinks?

- Do you drink before parties in order to feel okay about going?

- Do you drink to help you sleep?

- Are you annoyed when family or friends talk to you about your drinking?

- Do you drink because you feel tired, depressed, or worried?

- Do you hide your drinking from the people with whom you live?

- Do you drink alone?

- Do you have an occasional blackout or do you pass out? (Remember, a blackout is a loss of memory for a specific amount of time. It is *not* a passout or loss of consciousness.)

- Must you turn to alcoholic drink when you are disappointed or as a consolation or for celebration?

- Now, do you think you drink too much?

These are questions to be considered seriously, alone or with a friend or trained counselor. (They are not to be used as a party game that could give rise to guilty laughter.) If you have answered yes to even one of the checklist questions, you should consider making changes before the disease begins to hit you in more serious ways. A decision not to drink is a responsible and reasonable one. Giving up drinking or never starting to drink are both rational courses for people with alcoholic parents.

Even if you have decided that you do not have a problem and don't need to change your drinking habits, you can use this alcohol questionnaire periodically, much as you would go for a regular dental checkup or physical examination. You don't even have to consult your dentist or doctor for this one. It is free and painless and can reduce your chances of developing a fatal disease.

In a great many health matters, when you become aware of the risk of catching a disease, you have the opportunity to take the necessary steps to avoid it. Most people have been inoculated against smallpox; most have been immunized against typhoid fever, whooping cough, and polio. People take medication for malaria if they plan to visit a country that abounds in mosquitos carrying the disease. Prevention strategies are at the core of our public health system. They are based on the assumption that wiping out or averting disease is one goal of a civilized social system and that it is right, ethical, and humane to do everything possible to ward off crippling illnesses.

With alcoholism, primary prevention can begin with you; you can act as your own agent or advocate by testing yourself. If you have, in fact, recognized that there is a problem, you will not have to give up your own authority. Nor are you alone. No matter how you feel, you are not powerless in this situation. You may need help or encouragement, but you can make changes and choices.

Taking Matters into Your Own Hands

Take the case of Deedee, the daughter of two alcoholics. When she realized that her husband had a severe drinking problem, she became concerned with her own drinking. She knew she could easily slip into alcoholism because in high school she had had several blackouts. She also had had a difficult time giving up smoking and was only too aware of her willingness to use drugs when under stress. During the 1960s she had smoked a lot of pot, had experimented with other drugs, and still smoked a joint from time to time "just for fun."

Now she was feeling pressure from her husband to drink along with him. His friends and colleagues drank daily, stopping at bars after work on the way home. When Deedee's husband finally did get home he demanded that she join him "for a few." At first she acceded; she would even try to keep up with him, drink for drink. But after their child was born, she realized she became so groggy after a few beers she couldn't take care of the baby. (She thanked God the child was normal; she had done a lot of drinking during pregnancy.) She made a decision; she would not drink with her husband in the evenings unless someone else was there to help with the baby. He objected. He said she was being standoffish, overly concerned, and he felt personally rejected. It was not surprising that drinking became the source of tension between the two. As the strains mounted, Deedee consulted an alcoholism counselor who gave her some very good advice.

She was told, first, that she could understand more fully what was happening if she could distinguish between her husband's drinking problem and her own. The first counseling session was spent identifying the ways in which she and he differed in their relationship to liquor. Her husband did not recognize how the drinking was interfering with their life together, but she was fully aware of it. He would be so drunk before he got home that a coherent conversation was impossible. Her evenings, therefore, were lonely even though he was physically present. The counselor pointed out that she seemed able to go out and not drink; her husband could not (or would not) do that.

Later, Deedee and the counselor planned ways she could talk to her husband about the relationship between drinking and their deteriorating marriage. She would let him know that she was not going to drink with him and would not succumb to the pressure he was putting on her. She would also tell him that she thought he had a serious problem, that she was worried, and that she was going to begin attending Al-Anon meetings for help for herself.

Many times men and women like Deedee say, "I drank to keep him (or her) company and look where I ended up. I'm in AA now too." If you now live with an active alcoholic you may need to put extra energy into an awareness of your own drinking. Like many people in similar straits, you may find it worthwhile to talk to an alcoholism counselor or go to an Al-Anon meeting. In addition to learning more about alcoholism, you will learn practical ways to handle your own drinking. It may not be a problem for you now, but chances are you have concerns about it—even if you don't drink at all.

If you are living with a recently recovered alcoholic, it is helpful to keep in mind how tricky early sobriety can be. If you drink, you may want to give it up for a while, just out of consideration. Later it may not be of such crucial concern, and then you can make decisions about keeping alcoholic beverages in the house, drinking alone, celebrating with alcohol, and so on.

Other Compulsive Behaviors

Many adult children of alcoholics escape alcoholism but become involved with other substances—cocaine, opiates, sedatives, stimulants, hallucinogens, marijuana, or tobacco and caffeine. They become overeaters, workaholics, or serious gamblers. Too much television and compulsive exercising are also considered "volitional disorders," according to S. Joseph Mulé in *Behavior in Excess*. Anorexia nervosa (self-inflicted starvation), bulimia (forced vomiting after eating), and laxative abuse—all eating disorders with addictive qualities—are becoming more and more common, particularly among young people. Such behaviors may feel temporarily satisfying but are ultimately self-destructive. As the overweight daughter of an alcoholic puts it, "When I think no one loves me, I eat! I take care of myself by stuffing my face. In the end I hate myself because I just get fatter and fatter." Ironically, self-destructive behavior is sometimes used to shut out unbearable pain. It can be an attempt to control oneself or others, get attention, or make up for what was lacking in earlier life.

Does this mean that there is an addictive personality and that children of alcoholics run true to form? The answer is no. According to the National Research Council, no scientific study supports the theory that people who were orally deprived as infants, disciplined erratically, or had only one parent at home are any more likely than others to develop addictive or compulsive behavior. There is just no way to predict at this point who will or will not get "hooked." Still, it seems that the addictive personality does exist. The reason is that people who are addicted to one substance or form of behavior appear to be able to switch addictions, as a result of either their own internal discomfort or strong pressure from outside—a boss at work, a hounding family, a physician. Perhaps people who are addicted become more addictable.

A good many alcoholics, particularly women, become cross-addicted. They not only use alcohol but can go for any other sedative drug, often with just as much alacrity. Geraldine Delaney, director of Alina Lodge, an alcoholism recovery facility in Blairstown, New Jersey, gives a "pill talk" to every resident. As new clients come for treatment, she overturns their suitcases and has, over the years, emptied out thousands of vials filled with colorful pills, all brought in by patients who had come, ostensibly, to get the alcohol out of their systems.

Similarly, there are people who will use any "downer" available. And there are coffee freaks who will settle for any stimulant. So it goes.

There are times, though, when it is expedient to switch obsessions, particularly if the replacement is healthier and temporary. For example, many alcoholics who are drying out find that they begin to crave sweets. Since sugar is far less lethal than alcohol for most people, it seems perfectly fine to make that switch even at the risk of gaining weight. Ultimately the person who has switched will have to deal with the new compulsion. But chances are it won't be nearly as difficult as it was to stop drinking. People who stop smoking have said that they find chewing or sucking on a toothpick or lollipop provides them with alternative satisfaction.

Other people swear by jogging or square dancing, which may have the same function. They say it will get rid of tensions and make you feel high. They may be right. Research shows that the brain releases natural opiates (called endorphins) in response to pain. The theory is that jogging (or vigorous exercise) is uncomfortable enough to trigger the release of these substances, which are three times more powerful than morphine.

Frequently the substitute behavior seems to bear little relationship to the original habit. A woman who tried everything to stop smoking finally found that if she spent a good part of the day in the shower, she had to cut out cigarettes. There was no way she could light up under running water. An obese young man said, "Here's the way I do it: Each time I'm tempted to eat a box of Mallomar cookies before I get to the checkout counter, I summon up a picture of myself, thin, walking on a Caribbean beach. With the image in mind, I resolutely put the box back on the shelf." However, it is not so easy for most people. To find out about other ways to kick a habit, see Chapter 11, "Getting Help."

Uses and Abuses

One way people have chosen to work on their self-destructive behavior—particularly when they have escaped alcoholism but are stuck with something else—is to attend group therapy sessions or supportive group counseling. When life is plagued by behavior patterns that hang on no matter how hateful they are or what health hazards are involved, people decide to do anything to rid themselves of the habit. Just such desperation led a group of people, all with at least one alcoholic parent but all with their own obsessions, to meet weekly to explore solutions and help one another overcome the craving that torments them. This group of six women and two men get together each week to work on the problems that center around their own addictive behavior. Some are deeply disturbed over their tenacious habits, understandably so because of the health hazards involved; others accept their hangups and view them as preferable to alcoholism.

Tanya bites her fingernails; she's embarrassed when she looks at her raw fingertips. She remembers her mother's warnings— something to do with how she would eventually eat herself up. She also suffered when her mother put sharp mustard on her fingers. But it was to no avail; she continues to chew them down to the quick.

Danny is a compulsive shopper. Every time he feels low he

goes out and buys something for himself. His purchases range from a cheap necktie to a car with all the trappings. He really can't afford this kind of impulse buying, but he can't stop it. Fran says she stopped smoking when she became pregnant with her daughter, who is now four. But six months ago, when her mother developed throat cancer (an all too common occurrence in people who drink heavily and smoke), she picked up a cigarette and is now smoking two packs a day. She says that this is the one activity she and her mother enjoy together, but at the same time she procrastinates; she promises herself she will give up smoking when her mother is no longer there.

In George's family no one has experienced a tobacco-related illness. He has made a deliberate, though perhaps unwise, decision to continue smoking. He says he can't spend time with his family, (parents, brothers, sisters, and their families) and not smoke. The pressure from them to drink and smoke is too great to buck and they literally have thrown up a smokescreen that obliterates all awareness of the heavy drinking. However, George feels uneasy with his decision.

Elizabeth and Susan talk about their battle with food. Liz says she has been eating compulsively since she was six years old. At the first mention of food, six of the eight group members groan and say they too have "an eating problem."

Delia, for example, weighs eighty-five pounds and carries a low-calorie drink in her purse. She recognizes that her "weight problem" takes on a different form from the one the others experience. Not only does she sip liquids continually, but she makes a trip to the coffeepot every twenty minutes or so. After much talk about her need for a "heavy dose of caffeine," she discovered that the coffee she was drinking during meetings was caffeine-free. She was not tricked on purpose, but the result was that she found out she could do without her caffeine boost and that the trips to the coffeepot were for other reasons. For one thing, they had a placebo effect (swallowing anything would have worked); for another, perhaps the getting up and moving about made her less tense.

Surprisingly, and statistically unexpected, Sibyl is the only member of the group who is an alcoholic. She is sober and attends AA regularly, but as she puts it, "I smoke like a chimney and eat like a pig." Another group member chews gum incessantly. She comes in chomping; she leaves with the same piece in her mouth. When asked why she chews constantly, she says it relaxes her. No one has asked her for any further explanation.

Ben is a pill freak. He doesn't go in for hard drugs, mood changers, or anything obtainable only by prescription. However, he is never without a pocketful of pills—aspirin, nonprescription sleeping pills, antacids—and breath deodorizers. Once, when he got up, he left a small pile of assorted pills behind him on the chair and, like Hansel and Gretel's bread crumbs, a trail of pills on the floor as he walked across the room to the hall and stairs. At meetings he washes down a succession of pills, each with a mouthful of cold decaffeinated coffee. The group's reaction is one of mild amusement and understanding coupled with emphatic disapproval.

By group consensus, there is no smoking during meetings. Only after working together for many months did George bring up how angry this makes him feel. He was one of the first who noted the restlessness of group members who were denied their "pacifiers" during meetings. The smokers were feeling "antsy," as he put it, while the others carried on with gum chewing, coffee drinking, nail biting, and so on. Once he made this observation, it became clear to all that they were dealing with powerful forces that unleashed jealousy, envy, and annoyance.

Addictive behavior is sometimes identified as a personal adaptation to stress—great or small. Since all the members of the group described here have at least one parent who demonstrated, by example, that tension can be escaped through sedation with alcohol, they tend to escape through the same or a related hatch. They lack healthy models of how people learn to tolerate unpleasant internal feelings. Thus, their behavior often becomes self-destructive, causing them pain, disfigurement, or illness.

It may seem paradoxical, but all group members are profoundly interested in their own good health. Consequently, they have pledged to help one another get out of the addictive trap. They exchange telephone numbers and devote time each week, between sessions, to talking to one another and giving support and encouragement. Two of the smokers are investigating Smokenders and plan to go to a meeting together. The Overeaters Anonymous (OA) member has offered to take the still overeating member to a meeting.

If you are not in a group yourself, you may want to find a friend who belongs to a self-help group, or you may know someone who also wants to kick a habit. After all, this is how Alcoholics Anonymous began when Bill W. and Dr. Bob met to "share their experience, strength, and hope."

Since it appears that addictive behavior, in some form, is a common human experience, you shouldn't be surprised as the child of an alcoholic to find yourself a victim of what seems like irrational behavior—behavior that seems weird because you are doing something that you don't want to do and that you know isn't good for you.

At this time, there is no study that specifically examines the amount of substance abuse in the children of alcoholics and compares it to controls from nonalcoholic homes, but such a study could have important implications in terms of prevention, education, and treatment. It could become hard evidence to convince educators that alcohol education must be included in school curricula. It could convince alcoholic parents and grandparents that their offspring need special attention when it comes to drug and alcohol education. It could lead to special educative sessions for the children of addicts in mental health and correctional facilities. And it could sensitize us to the vulnerabilities of children who have lived with parents addicted to any substance. Such a study could alert us to populations that might be subjected to child abuse and/or neglect and to children who may be in need of mental health services. In other words, we need to *pay attention* to the children and grandchildren of alcoholics so they will have a better chance.

6

Marriage and Closeness— for Better or for Worse

As a kid I would sit at the dinner table and tell myself, "I'm not here. Someday I'll have candle-light, conversation and love." All that's still a fig-ment of my imagination. I don't have any of it—yet.

Jeff, Age 35

It does seem to be extraordinarily difficult for children of alcohol-ics to make long-term commitments, marriage included. Fanta-sies can get in the way of dealing with the tough realities, and the same personality characteristics that complicate friendships and daily living also complicate the delicate business of finding the right person and helping the marriage survive. This is tricky enough for anyone—and there is no fail-safe recipe. But children of alcoholics have special concerns. If you have seen only an out-of-focus picture, how do you know what a good marriage looks like? If you have been so involved with your parents that you have never built a life of your own, where do you start? How can you keep from repeating the chaotic pattern you grew up with? It isn't easy, but it can be done.

All is not doom and gloom. There is no conclusive evidence that children of alcoholics are any more likely than anyone else to form unhappy liaisons. Sometimes, in fact, working to overcome handicaps leads to stronger ties. Sometimes a second try is needed to make marriage work. And some good marriages are like mira-cles, for no one will ever know how or why they came about.

There are many ways to form relationships but children of alcoholics tend to choose from a limited number of possibilities. You may find your own experience echoed in them.

For Better or Worse

In looking for the love and closeness they missed as children, some people confuse physical contact or sexual involvement with emotional warmth. They therefore become promiscuous, but get little satisfaction from their sexual wanderings. For them, true devotion to another human being is too much of a gamble so they enter relationships that can't possibly last.

On the other hand, there are those who can't tolerate being alone at all and therefore cling to friends, relatives, and just about anyone who happens to be around. In both friendships and love relationships, instead of breaking up when things go sour they remain attached and dependent. A homosexual man was so terrified of being alone that as he fought to hang on to his current lover he also practiced imagining what it was like to sleep in a bed with no one there beside him, hoping to prepare himself.

Sometimes it seems that when that fear of loneliness becomes too great, present-day relationships become compulsive and the equivalent of what alcohol is for the alcoholic. "I keep going back to this guy and he keeps beating me up," says a saleswoman in her thirties. She stays long after there is nothing to stay for, in a kind of distorted loyalty. Perhaps it is the same sort of loyalty she saw in her own parents, who stuck together despite the discord.

She may also keep going back for another reason: the fear of change. Children of alcoholics have learned that change is not for the better. Anxiety about the unknown immobilizes them. This affects not only their relationships but their daily living. Any switch—a rained-out picnic or a canceled appointment—will bring on hours of internal despair because these events are experienced as reenactments of scenes from a helpless childhood. If they can be recognized for what they are in the present, they become less threatening, for they are certainly a part of what everyone experiences. So the overreaction (and the sticking with an unsuitable partner) is based on a memory of the past rather than on the facts of today.

Saying Maybe; Saying No

The past often intrudes. When he was six years old, Daniel's mother left his alcoholic father to bring up her two children alone. Five years later she married again and the boys had a stable family life for a dozen years. Their biological father was in the picture occasionally in the early years, but then disappeared from their lives. Daniel talks of him as "my mother's first husband." Daniel has had several live-in loving relationships but no long-term commitments. The shadowy figure of an alcoholic father who slipped in and out of his life is still lurking in the background, making him wary of giving himself fully to anyone.

Some children of alcoholism avoid this hesitation by concluding from the start that they will not marry at all. The daughter of two alcoholics told her boyfriend, "I will never get married and that's that." He told her she was crazy. "What's the matter with you?" he asked. Even though they had known each other for years, he couldn't really understand how life had been for her as she struggled with her parents, who were wrapped together in a tight knot of conspiracy and suspicion. In fact, he could hardly believe the stories she had told him—of having been pushed down the stairs, of being kept awake at night by her mother's drunken complaints, of hearing her father singing so loudly in the hallway outside their apartment that neighbors couldn't ignore him. Despite the fact that this young woman needed someone to take care of her, someone to help her distinguish right from wrong, and even someone to help her choose clothing, the uncertainties involved in a permanent relationship (which might include having children) were too great. What she had seen as she grew up was not her idea of how things should be, but she had no idea how to do things any other way.

Even parents who do not provide such a distorted and inadequate model can complicate the question of marriage for their children. Many parents (those who are not alcoholic as well as those who are) can't permit their children to form close relationships outside the family circle. They may be so vulnerable themselves that they feel safe only by keeping a child on their laps long after the child is ready to get up and go. The child then does not develop a way to relate to others when the proper time comes and is stuck or unable to separate. For example, some parents cradle their infants in their arms constantly, even when the children would much rather be allowed to explore the space in which they live. Other parents push their children to walk when they can hardly straighten out their legs. The tuned-in parent is the one who will take cues from children, not push or pull but allow them to grow up at their own pace and in their own time. When children are allowed to develop only within parental time schedules, their capacity to form relationships away from home is made more difficult from the start.

Then there are those children who have been overly involved (often with good reason) with their families over long periods of time. They feel both uneasy and guilty when they try to create families of their own and often wait years before attempting marriage. They use all sorts of distancing devices: "I became a well-developed smartass. Believe me, that kept people away," said a young stockbroker who stayed tied to his parents while he waited for someone to come along and love him. Others manage to delay making any permanent commitments because they are afraid of making a mistake. They don't trust their judgment, for they have already gone down the wrong path too often.

Just Like Dear Old Dad (or Mom)

The wrong path frequently leads to the daughters of alcoholic fathers marrying alcoholics. (One estimate is as high as 60 percent. Men less frequently re-create their families of origin.) In some women this pattern is so strong that they divorce one alcoholic husband and marry another, often very quickly. They fall into the trap unconsciously and in spite of firm determination never to become involved with another alcoholic man. Women are usually surprised and baffled, often devastated, at having unwittingly repeated the pattern their mothers began. They say that at the time they married they didn't realize they were falling in love with someone who was drinking too much. Often the pathological drinking hadn't begun at the time the couple began to plan for their future and the potential problem wasn't easy to spot. Some young people call off marriage plans when they realize what's actually going on. But it may take a long time for that realization to come because at home a woman may have learned to tolerate all kinds of outrageous behavior and to put up with much more than is conceivably acceptable to people who haven't lived with alcoholic insanities that pass for rationality.

Another possibility is that the woman doesn't recognize different drinking styles. A father may have been a binge drinker who was sober a lot of the time, whereas a husband-to-be may be one of those people who remain "a little drunk" all the time. Or the woman may never have experienced the early stages of alcoholism in a parent, particularly if she was among the younger children in the family. And chances are she can't recognize that a boyfriend's drinking is excessive and different or on its way toward escalation. As one woman admitted, "I never fell in love with anyone who was sober when I met him."

Then, too, the family pattern may be repeated because it is familiar, and a way of identifying with a long-suffering mother. "I married an alcoholic," reported another woman. "I married him because I didn't realize there was any different way of being. When we were going out, he'd never show up on time, but what's new? I didn't even know it could be any other way. With my father always sloshed, who was ever on time?" She had been fond of her alcoholic father and saw in her husband the good qualities she had loved, as well as the less admirable behavior.

There are many women like her. Whatever the reasons, they find themselves saddled with sick husbands. They feel let down, betrayed, angry, isolated, and afraid. One of their biggest fears is that their own drinking may escalate. By now they may have children. They may have careers they value a lot. They probably saw awful things happen when they were younger and living with their parents. And they have always known and repeated to themselves what Claudia Black used as the title for her book about children of alcoholics: *It Can't Happen to Me.* And now it is happening.

The Search for the Dream

Some people cling to the old fantasy that they will be able to change or rescue the person they love. They need to feel needed, have had a lot of practice trying to rescue people, and have a hidden urge to continue that kind of behavior. Alice, just seventeen, is already involved with a young man she is trying to save. She came home one evening and told her mother she had been to an Al-Anon meeting and had found it "very interesting." Her mother, a staunch member of a local group, was overjoyed, gave her daughter a hug, and told her how happy she was that she was finally going to learn something about alcoholism and begin to understand her father better. The young girl looked at her mother somewhat sheepishly. "No, mom, you don't get it. You see, that new guy I'm seeing gets bombed every time we go out and I don't like what's happening between us. I went to Al-Anon to try to clear up some problems he and I have been having."

Another familiar fantasy that gets in the way of realistic relationships is that of finding the "and they lived happily ever after" mate. A woman who has had three messy marriages says her alcoholic father wrecked her chances of choosing a suitable husband. If a man was not perfect he seemed as inadequate as her father. "All little girls grow up with a vision of Prince Charming," she explains, "but most also have human fathers who make mistakes, trip up once in a while, and correct this dream. My father was so unpredictable. Sometimes he really was Prince Charming and other times he was the Devil. The image was never corrected. Now, if the men I love aren't perfect, they seem as ineffectual as my father was." She keeps searching for the cloud-built person who doesn't exist and rejecting the real-life men who are only human.

The Shell Game

To protect themselves, children of alcoholics often develop a hard shell. This serves two purposes: It keeps them from being hurt and it keeps other people at a distance. Getting close is threatening, scary, and replete with implications that they may ultimately have to pay for the closeness in the same way they did as children. Yet they also want to lean on others. Sometimes both emotions are experienced simultaneously, and the ambivalence of wanting and not wanting closeness creates immobilizing confusion. "I'm always on guard," says a forty-year-old man. "I'm afraid I'll be swallowed up, devoured, if I let someone love me." On the other hand, when these people love someone, they love utterly. "They want to fuse with the loved one as their mother fused with them," explains a New York psychotherapist, "and often the other partner can't stand it and gets out. Then they find themselves abandoned and alone again, because they have never learned to let other people support, protect, or help them."

Betty is one of those young women who won't trust anyone to be there to catch them if they trip. "I haven't told my husband about my miscarriage," she confides. "I don't want to upset him." By keeping quiet and choosing to suffer alone with the loss, she has effectively created a gap between herself and the person who should be sharing her sadness. Patterns of dishonesty and withholding information automatically destroy intimacy so that chances of true emotional closeness become slim.

Betty had learned early from her alcoholic mother that anger, joy, love, fear, and all other feelings had to go unacknowledged. So how was she going to talk openly to her husband? She was afraid he would reject or judge her, as her mother had. What Betty has done is transfer the expectations she had of her mother onto her present-day situation (her husband), and she is still unable to separate the two. When children grow up, they expect to be treated as they were treated when they were young. If they were abused, ignored, betrayed, or used, they expect their spouse or loved one to do the same. And, in response, they tend to project onto the current important person in their lives feelings they had toward their parents.

Low Man (or Woman) on the Totem Pole

Children of alcoholism may accept the critical feelings their parent expressed toward them or may assume there is something inside them (perhaps an image of their alcoholic parent) that is corrupt or rotten and unlovable. They feel vulnerable and expect to be quickly discarded so the familiar feeling—a need to stay clear and isolated—returns.

If people have a low self-image and feel inadequate when it comes to setting limits, it will be easy for them to make an error by becoming involved with someone whom they don't really respect or who is unsuitable in some crucial way. The child of an alcoholic may not feel worthy of anyone better, but in the long run a relationship of this sort doesn't work out for either partner. One feels unloved and unappreciated; the other feels disappointed, angry, and even more worthless.

Saying Yes Too Soon

Feeling worthless and desperate in an intolerable home situation may lead to seeing marriage (or pregnancy and then marriage) as a way to escape. The consequences of hasty marriages and of premature parenthood can be disastrous. The younger the mother, the more likely her baby is to get a poor start in life. Birth weight and chances of survival are lower; social and economic problems soar. However, like most people, adult children of alcoholics strive to be like everyone else. Often that need is exaggerated. One woman said, "I got married because I wanted to look right. If you have a house, a husband, a baby, everything is fine." She had learned from her mother that if things *look* good, they *are* good. Later on, unfortunately, she realized she didn't know how marriage should look. "Now I feel as if marriage is a play I've always wanted to star in, but I've never seen it performed and no one has given me a script."

Walking the Sexual Tightrope

A missing script may also be involved in the development of sexual identity. No one knows just how a child learns to be comfortable or uncomfortable with masculinity or femininity, but it is possible to look at some variations on the theme at work in alcoholic families. A sexual identity problem is like a branch growing out of the issue of identity itself. The alcoholic's perception of his or her child is clouded by the actions of the drug; this blurred image is reflected onto the child, and the lack of clarity makes it difficult for the young person to emerge as a separate, clearly defined individual. Then, too, because the parent can be so different at different times, there is no cohesive whole for a child to take in. The child may reject or deny the irrational behavior yet be afraid of being just like the unpredictable parent.

One man explained it this way: "One of the problems with alcoholic parents is that their personal borders are fuzzy and they live that way. When they drink, the boundaries appear to dissolve between their thoughts and their feelings, making thinking processes pretty muddy. That's exactly what has happened to me. When I try to define who 'I' am, and where 'I' am, I might as well be everywhere. In a way, I'm numbed out, just like my mother, just as if I were the one doing the drinking."

Studies of children of alcoholics have come up with conflicting findings about the effect of an alcoholic model (parent) on sexual identity. One study reports no greater gender confusion in these children than in the general population. Another maintains that the child of the same sex will have the most difficulty; yet another says it will be the child of the opposite sex.

Parent and Child: Same Sex

First, let's look at what might happen to the same-sex child. Keep in mind, though, that all human beings are different and that these interactions are only possibilities, not certainties. At some point in childhood little girls want to be "just like mommy" and little boys "just like daddy." But a girl with an alcoholic mother sees a confusing and often inadequate picture, as does a boy with an alcoholic father. Both will take something from each parent, alcoholic or not. The girl may have seen her mother trying to get a spoon into the baby's mouth when she was so drunk she couldn't do it. The boy may have seen his alcoholic father so belittled that being like him carries with it the chance of annihilation. At best, the child's understanding of who he or she is is a shaky one. This shakiness may extend to uncertainty about maleness and femaleness.

There are many theories of how people develop one sexual identity or another. One holds that homosexuality may be the result of an unclear picture of sexuality in the parents which is then unconsciously adopted by the child. Another theory claims that a child who did not get what he or she needed emotionally from the parent of the same sex will seek that love from a same-sex partner. Most often, of course, the child maintains a heterosexual identity, with perhaps some conflicts that mirror those of the parent.

Alcoholic men may not be completely comfortable with their masculinity. The murky image they present to their sons may push the sons into rebellion or rejection. Boys often rebel with delinquent behavior; girls may choose other means. The daughter of an always stunningly dressed alcoholic woman says, "I wanted to be everything my mother was not. She made me have a permanent at twelve and wear lipstick. She even wanted me to wear pearls to school! I hated it, so I became a slob, just the opposite of what she was like. I would never go shopping with her for clothes, and I picked my best sweater out of someone's trash." Another woman says, "My mother was so miserable I was afraid of being a woman. When I started to menstruate I hid it and I tried to think of myself as 'neuter.' " A man remembers: "One day my father would be loving and the next day he would hit me with his belt. One month he was working, the next month he would not come home at all." The inconsistency made it hard for this man to know what he should be. And yet, a Los Angeles marriage counselor comments, "I've never had a male client who rejected his alcoholic father as a gender model, but I've had several women who did not want to be women because their alcoholic mother seemed so downtrodden. Society still sees a woman who drinks too much as beneath contempt, but a drinking man may keep the aura of drinking as being 'macho,' particularly if he continues to support his family."

But even if the male alcoholic holds on to his job, his masculinity at home may be in question, so everyone in the household will be subjected to the sounds of bitter fighting centered around sex. One of the common results of too much alcohol is impotence. Children report hearing, "What's the point of sleeping with you anyhow?" or "You stink, and I'm not going to bed with you until you shape up."

Often the male alcoholic is kept firmly outside the family circle. Even after he sobers up, it is hard for him to get back in. The other members don't trust him—he may begin drinking again; he's already made thousands of unkept promises. And the family system works smoothly as long as he is kept out. A boy may wonder if the "outsider" position is the one he wants to find himself in when he grows up. And a girl may wonder, "Is this what I want to be married to?"

When the wife is the alcoholic, the husband may find another woman. This, too, inevitably leads to arguments for all to hear. When a girl sees her mother deceived, she finds it hard to look forward to life with a man. If there is actual physical violence, the uncertainty is compounded for both son and daughter. The girl may have trouble all her life relating to men, and the boy, puzzled about what normal male behavior is, may stay clear of heterosexual relationships.

Parent and Child: Opposite Sex

Now let's look at what might happen to the opposite-sex child, again keeping in mind that these are generalizations that may or may not apply to your specific circumstances. It is not only the child of the same sex as the alcoholic who may have problems developing a definite gender identification or who may have problems relating to the opposite sex as an adult. When the alcoholic is the more loving and giving parent, as happens frequently, he or she and the child of the opposite sex may turn to each other for emotional sustenance—a warmth they don't get from the non-drinking but colder parent. This can lead to difficulties in later life, particularly if the closeness leads to incest. Even if it doesn't, a daughter may be afraid of getting involved with men because of the guilt she feels about her forbidden attachment to her father. Loving a man can be dangerous, and she may then turn to women as love objects. Or she may have difficulty replacing her father— that is, finding a man who will make her feel as good as he did.

In some cases, sexual identity is ill defined because a child feels more like his or her alcoholic parent of the opposite sex and rejects the parent of the same sex. A young man says that as a boy he was told, "You're just like your mother." In college he would "wake up and feel I *was* my mother. When I discovered I was gay I wanted to kill myself. It meant to me that I would never escape an unhealthy lifestyle even though I don't drink. Homosexuality and alcoholism have a lot in common—the hiding, the shame, and society's attitudes."

The effects of parental alcoholism on gender identity is still unexplored in the world of the single parent. Some studies show that men are more likely to leave an alcoholic woman than vice versa. And today's divorce statistics indicate that many children of alcoholics are brought up in homes in which only the mother is present. No one has looked at what happens to children in this case, but the potential for calamity is real because children are at the mercy of their only parent-in-residence. If that parent is drinking, is unreliable, or is not there consistently, the hazards are multiplied.

Certainly, not all children in alcoholic homes emerge with uncertain or conflicted feelings about their sexuality or about marriage. Most are secure in the reality that they are either men or women and go beyond sexual stereotypes to be comfortable with some of the attributes with which society tags the opposite sex. They may have problems with intimacy, but these seem to be endemic in today's world and not confined to people with alcoholic parents.

Second Chance

Like so many other people today, children of alcoholics often struggle through one unhappy marriage, survive the tensions of divorce, and go on to a second, happy marriage. What they learned in the first relationship helps them deal with the vicissitudes of the second. Joyce first married a man who needed her— her money, that is. The money she lent him went into gambling rather than into his business and the marriage failed when the business did. Joyce's present husband is not so unreliable. She can trust him and he can listen to her—which is what Joyce needs most.

Some second tries involve husbands or wives who met each other at AA meetings, where as children of alcoholics they were working to overcome their own compulsive drinking. "I finally feel loved and understood," the daughter of an alcoholic father says. "We can give each other what we never got at home, or in our first marriages." Of course, second marriages are not the only way. Happiness is hidden in all sorts of unexpected places, if you have the courage to look and the will to change.

7

You and
Your Children

Being a parent is the cruncher—kids are so
chancy. That's what I can't take.

Josh, Age 43

If you've had the courage to commit yourself to marriage and a
family of your own, you may now be faced with the awesome responsibilities of parenthood. For you, they may be especially
anxiety-provoking, since you know that alcoholism is a family illness. It not only affects members of the nuclear family but also
shows up in aunts, uncles, nieces, nephews, and cousins. It may
skip a generation and reappear in a grandchild. But once deviant
ways of using alcohol have been established, those inappropriate
responses tend to be carried down from generation to generation.
As your children grow up you may recognize in them inclinations
that will worry you and continue to remind you of your heritage
and theirs.

"I knew Greg would be an alcoholic from the time he was a
baby," said the mother of a twenty-five-year-old. "He gulped his
bottle from the very beginning. Later he would grab his cup of
milk and pour it down his throat. He loved the first sip of his father's beer and cried for more. As a small boy he would finish any
drink, alcoholic or not, that happened to be left out. As he grew up
I became more and more upset. I knew disasterville was on its
way."

Greg's mother highlighted an important question: Are some people born with the tendency to become alcoholic? The answer at this point is a tentative yes, although the signs Greg's mother saw are not necessarily the important ones, and no one is fated, inevitably, to become addicted to alcohol. But the evidence for some sort of genetic link in alcoholism is piling up, so Greg's mother was understandably concerned.

Using her own unreliable "markers" as warning signals, she was terrified that her son could easily follow in the footsteps of her own father, who had died of the disease. She would warn Greg, "You watch out or you're going to end up just like my father." (Families sometimes write their own scripts.) Eventually she took matters into her own hands and made an exaggerated effort to avoid what she thought was practically inevitable. First, she learned as much as possible about alcohol and alcoholism. Then, as Greg grew up, she talked to him on every possible (and impossible) occasion about what had happened in her own family and why she was so concerned about any kind of drinking. She also told him in how many ways he reminded her of her alcoholic father. These topics were difficult for her to talk about, but she felt an obligation to explain the origins of her fears. In spite of her efforts—or perhaps because of the pressure of her overconcern—the event she had so feared occurred when Greg was thirteen. He came home one night, obviously very drunk, and reeled through the living room and up the front stairs. His mother did not take it calmly. She lit into him, grounded him for a month, cried, and concluded that all her efforts had gone down the drain. She asked herself, "Did it have to happen?"

Actually, nothing had "happened" other than the fact that Greg had gotten drunk, an event that is inordinately commonplace. There are very few people who have not had too much to drink at least once in their lives. However, Greg's oversensitive mother had a colossal emotional investment in her son's sobriety, so the punishment she inflicted on him was far more severe than necessary. Not until her husband rather abruptly brought it to her attention did she realize how inappropriate her response was. This had been the first time Greg had had too much to drink. But she could not tolerate any drunken behavior at all.

Another mother, the daughter of an alcoholic, reacted to her son's drinking spree in a completely different way. She ignored it.

When he was escorted home by a friend, ran a zigzag course to the bathroom, threw up, and spent the following day in bed, she said nothing. She could not face the fact that her child had had too much to drink, and she simply avoided the obvious, asked him casually if he'd had a good time at his friend's party, and pointed out that he seemed to have lost a shoe.

There are many parents like this, children of alcoholics, who are unable to talk about drinking with their own children. The topic is too loaded with memories and painful feelings. They handle their concern by ignoring, denying, or accepting drunkenness as "normal" even when it is repeated in a continuing pattern. Neither Greg's mother nor the denying mother is to be blamed. Nor are their reactions extraordinary. Each represents a personal style or way of coping with the problem. Both will need to develop more rational attitudes toward drunkenness so their children will not, in turn, grow up with warped views about drinking.

Edith's Story

You can't count on time, either, to eradicate ingrained emotionality. Sixty-year-old Edith realizes that her mother's alcoholism has deeply affected her attitude toward her own children. She has never been able to rid herself of the deep fear she carries with her, not so much for herself now, for she has lived a good part of her life without a drinking problem, but for her children. One weekend, her son, his wife, and their two little boys came to visit. After dinner, her husband offered brandy to the adults. The offer certainly was not unusual; Edith and her husband always served after-dinner drinks whenever people visited. "When my son said, 'Yes, I'd like one,' my heart stopped. I felt for his life and even though I know better, I could not control the irrational gut feeling that any drinking leads to alcoholism."

The effects of alcoholism are certainly multigenerational and get handed down in attitudes no matter what people know. The overwhelming sense of fear felt by so many adult children of alcoholics is often free-floating, obscure in its origins. But when you hear a story like Edith's the genesis of her anxiety becomes clear, particularly when she describes her unpredictable parents and their self-indulgence. You don't have to wonder why she still cringes when the drinks are passed around. Even though you may recognize how your own fears grew out of family disharmony, you may still have to review and continue looking at early painful events so that the attitudes you transmit to your children are not as emotionally tainted as Edith's. Your heart does not have to stop, as hers does, when you see your children drink; they will not gain by your overreaction to their drinking.

Should We Have Children?

Some children of alcoholics are so fearful of repeating the mistakes of the past that they hesitate to have children at all. "How can I bring up a child?" a young student asks. "I don't know how to do it. My mother didn't know which end was up when I was a kid."

Other people tackle the uncertainties of parenting by becoming rigidly controlling. "The rules were always changing in my family. I never knew what to expect or what was expected of me," one mother put it. Now, she is determined that her own children will behave according to clear, strict standards. In reacting to her own concern about control, she has been making unrealistic demands on her children, insisting on rigid curfews, homework every night from 7:00 to 9:00, and very little time for relaxed fun.

She is also afraid that any emotion—laughter, fear, crying—will run riot unless it is quickly squelched. What she had learned to beware of at home was that the expression of feelings could change with frightening unpredictability from good humor to excoriating anger, from laughter to tears. Now she is becoming aware that she is overreacting to her own children's normal mood swings. Like her, you may be concerned that you will carry over inappropriate attitudes. But you can learn other ways of behaving.

Parenting Can Be Learned Too

You may ask yourself, "Why do I have to learn how to be a parent? It's supposed to come naturally." You sense that your own parents weren't very good at the job, and you don't want to repeat the same mistakes. Your anxieties may stem directly from the fear of repeating the pattern of your alcoholic parent; or if you are one of those who cannot drink safely, you may worry about transmitting your problem directly to your children.

Whether you realize it or not, you already know a lot about parenting. One way you have come to know about it is through identification. We all absorb unconsciously aspects of other people's behavior, characteristics, and attitudes. (More consciously, we imitate or copy.) Every child identifies, to a greater or lesser degree, with the parent of the same sex. Thus children learn skills without being taught. For instance, they learn language by imitating. But they learn attitudes—their parents beam when they take their first steps; their parents expect them to assert their rights—by identification.

Where will you look outside yourself for healthy parenting models and information so that you will feel a measure of confidence in yourself as a parent or parent-to-be? Your greatest and closest resource—one that is so obvious it is sometimes overlooked—is your spouse. You can add to your understanding in other ways:

- Read about parenting. All libraries and bookstores have how-to books on bringing up children.

- Talk to friends, neighbors, and relatives. Watch them and find out how they set curfews, what their children do after school, and how they talk to them.

- Recall the good things about your own parents.

- Call to mind the parents you most admired when you were a child. (One girl dreamed that her aunt was really her mother because she was so loving and accepting.)

- Begin to try to trust yourself and your instincts; they may be the best teacher.

Remember that every child is an experimental case and that everyone has concerns about being an adequate parent. After you have read some books, talked to friends, and observed the child-rearing practices going on around you, you may want to take part in more formal learning. Many communities have neighborhood centers, community colleges, and so on where parent groups meet to learn from one another or from professional leaders. Some towns have community-based groups for new parents. It may take some effort on your part to locate the most appropriate one for you, but with a few telephone calls or a look at local newspapers you should be able to find what you are looking for. You may be surprised to discover how many people have also lived with alcoholic parents, share many of the same experiences, and have the same residual fears and concerns.

Talking to Your Children about Alcohol

For most parents, talking to children about alcohol isn't any more difficult than discussing any loaded topic such as sex, politics, money, religion, or the nuclear bomb. For you, though, alcohol has a special meaning and is therefore hard to talk about. But you can't renege and leave it up to someone else. Just by omission, your children will wonder. And they will probably want to know what you think.

Even when they are very young, your children may notice that you are touchy on the subject. They may have seen you flinch as a friend poured a drink, or they may have noticed that you rush them by when a drunk person is on the street. You may think you're being dispassionate, but children are perceptive and they pick up subtleties. They will detect your feelings even when you try to disguise them or appear neutral. It is better for you as a parent to make your views on alcohol known rather than to cover them up, because in spite of your efforts to the contrary your personal values, fears, and attitudes, much like your style of dress and your characteristic gestures, will invariably come through. Try to work toward a relationship with your child or children in which all views can be recognized and safely expressed. An open dialogue should include listening to one another and respecting each other's opinions without being judgmental.

Young children of elementary school age are interested in what drinks have alcohol in them and why drunk people "act funny." They have a tremendous curiosity about drunk people, who usually seem frightening. In this case, as with others, the element of fear is somehow enticing. (Children challenge each other with suggestions like "Let's go up in the attic and get scared.")

One young father, the son of an alcoholic, simply could not deal forthrightly with his six-year-old's anxious curiosity about a drunkard they passed walking along the street. The besotted man reeled along, careening from the gutter to the store fronts and back again. When asked, "What's wrong with that man, daddy?" the father replied, "He didn't take his nap this afternoon."

Unvarnished honesty is better than this kind of charming evasion, particularly as children grow up and become more interested in the psychological and physiological consequences of drinking. Their interest will be determined largely by what's going on with their peers, and they will begin experimenting with alcoholic beverages. That could happen at home (many alcoholics say they got started as children by finishing off drinks left on a living room table after a party), or it could happen with friends and in secret. At some point between ages ten and fifteen most children have an experimental bout with alcohol. So *don't push the panic button.*

One young high school student told his guidance counselor about his mother's overconcern, which had backfired: "Every time my mother finds out that I had a drink she gets hysterical and says I'm going to become an alcoholic just like her father was. She tries to drag me to therapists, and once she got me to an AA meeting. If she's going to do all this, I may as well enjoy myself." And this young boy did continue to "enjoy himself" until the day he smashed up the family car.

The chances of your teenagers developing problems with alcohol will be vastly diminished if they feel free to talk to you about what they're doing, why they are doing it, and how it makes them feel. As with younger children, the element of secrecy adds glamour to the act. A feeling of being grown up is central to adolescent transitional behavior, so discussing alcohol out in the open, during supper table conversation or while driving, may make a casual but significant connection between you and your children. It will be easier if your family is accustomed to discussing serious matters on a regular basis. When a family whose dinner table talk is usually about who's going to do what chore or who took more than her share of the hot rolls suddenly starts talking about drinking, a discussion of alcohol may seem jolting.

It is important to start thinking about the content and quality of communication in your family when the children are young. You will have to push yourself to face the facts, use real words for the real things, and at the same time not transmit the intensity of your feelings to your children. And it's certainly best to talk about drinking before children have made peer commitments. Once they've hooked up with a drinking or pill-popping crowd, it will be much more difficult to get to them.

As time goes on there will be a natural and understandable flow of ideas geared to your family as it matures. One important point: When you discuss drinking, help your children realize there are choices to be made and that deciding not to drink is a viable one. Remember, too, that what you do is at least as important as what you say. According to Ellen Morehouse of the Westchester County (New York) Department of Community Mental Health: "Parents' drinking patterns are the single most important factor in determining how children drink."

When You Talk to Your Children about Alcohol

- *Talk to them when they have a need to know.* The time may be different from when you have a need to tell them. For instance, when you have just returned from a visit to your alcoholic father, his problem may be uppermost in your mind. But your child may be trying to get ready for school, matching skirt to sweater or finding last night's homework. This will not be the time for you to discuss the effect of drinking on behavior.

- *Know the facts.* Don't get caught making vague or unsupportable statements that may only be "a little bit true."

- *Don't confuse your children by ignoring what they are capable of learning at a given age.* If you give them information that is too complicated, they'll lose interest very quickly

- *Never talk down to your children.* They'll know it and they'll turn off.

- *Don't take a "holier than thou" or "I know better, you will learn" attitude.* Both of these will be received as another turn-off.

- *Use language that you are at ease with.* Don't change your vocabulary just because you're talking to your children. They may use "ripped," "buzzed," or "stoned." You still can use "drunk" or whatever comes naturally to you.

- *Avoid being a bore or lecturing.*

- It's easy to become a monomaniac. Your children will let you know if you're going in that direction. "Hey, dad, you're not bringing up that alcohol stuff again!" might be a tip to you to change the subject.

- *Listen to yourself.* See if you always mention alcohol or alcoholism at times when it is unnecessary to refer to either. For example, a father might say, "Let's go to the burger place for supper—they don't serve alcoholic beverages there." Or a mother might say, "Set the table with the tall glasses. I don't like those little ones, they look like wine glasses." (Adult children of alcoholics, like alcoholics themselves, are likely to bring up the topic of drinking even when it is not pertinent.)

- *Try to be clear about your own attitudes and feelings.* Let your children know your real values about alcohol use and why you want them to wait until they are older. They need to learn when they are young how to cope with stress and boredom and how to socialize without using chemicals.

- *Help your children connect the dangers of drinking with driving.* If you are out to dinner you might point out, "Daddy is not drinking because he's driving us home." Or, if you usually have a drink at dinner time, you may not be doing so one night because you are driving to the movies later.

- *Remind children that alcohol will not make you pretty, popular, rich, or famous.* When you watch TV shows or commercials about alcohol, you may want to comment on the advertising.

- *Remember that peer pressure often starts early.* You have undoubtedly heard, "But everyone else is doing it"—whether it's pierced ears or certain kinds of clothes or hairstyles. This is a topic that can be discussed with your children at very young ages. Parent support groups are helpful in establishing community policy on drinking, driving, curfews, and all issues where children rely on peers to establish norms. With the backing of other parents, you can be more confident about the policies your own family sets.

- *Have faith, particularly if it is warranted, in your children's judgment and ability to use alcohol in responsible ways.* Children act more responsibly when they feel you trust them.

• *Remember that it's okay to say you don't know the answer to a question.* You will maintain more credibility with your children if you let them know that there are times when you don't have the answers. (They may enjoy researching the subject along with you.)

Debunking the Myths

To correct some of the misinformation that young people pick up as conventional wisdom, you may want to do some educating at home. Here are some of the most serious myths to dispel:

1.   *Alcohol is an aid to sexual prowess.* Young people especially will boast of conquests made when under the influence of liquor. Young women will blame an unwanted pregnancy on "going too far" because of too much drinking; young men will attribute their ability to "make out" with a woman to the beers that loosened inhibitions.

The *fact* is that one or two drinks may lower inhibitions, but drinking to excess has a negative effect on sexual performance and can ultimately lead to atrophy of the sex glands and the lack of ability to perform. Shakespeare knew it when he wrote in *Macbeth* that drink "provokes the desire, but takes away the performance."

2.   *Alcohol warms you up.* Even in the face of prohibition in the 1920s and 1930s a flask of straight whiskey was considered a necessity at any outdoor sports event, particularly a cool fall football game; the traditional Saint Bernard carries brandy to the chilled mountain climber; and these days skiers are portrayed coming out of the cold to a hot alcoholic toddy.

The *fact* is that alcohol actually lowers body temperature and that drinking in very cold weather can be dangerous. It makes you feel warmer, but that feeling is only temporary and the end result of a snort in the cold is to make you colder.

3.   *You can drive better after a drink or two.* This is probably *the* most dangerous myth about alcohol. Eradicating it could save your life.

The *fact* is that you may feel more relaxed after a drink and you may feel *as if* you are driving better, but you are not! Vision, judgment, and reaction time are seriously impaired by the action of alcohol on the brain. There are no exceptions; it is true of everyone.

4. *You can't overdose on alcohol the way you can on other drugs.* People don't realize that eating or drinking too much of anything too rapidly will result in death.

The *fact* is that alcohol is a central nervous system depressant and when taken in large doses can cause such extensive neurological damage that the heart will stop and the respiratory center in the brain will cease functioning. Young, naïve drinkers, drinking for kicks or on dares, are the most vulnerable. They are found in hospital emergency rooms having their stomachs pumped. The problem lies in the fact that alcohol is absorbed into the bloodstream so rapidly that often the damage is done before medical help can be obtained. Alcohol overdose causes more deaths in young people than any other drug, including heroin.

5. *There is something different about beer or wine—they are not as lethal as hard liquor.* Some alcoholic people will say, "I only drink beer," as if there were no alcohol in it. People feel free to give their children a sip of beer or wine but not a sip of any hard liquor. In some tropical countries beer is cheaper than a cola drink and is used interchangeably with it.

The *fact* is that a twelve-ounce can of beer, a five-ounce glass of wine, and a one-and-a-half-ounce shot glass of 80-proof whiskey all contain the same amount of alcohol. As the National Institute on Alcohol Abuse and Alcoholism points out on a poster: "If you drink a lot of beer, you drink a lot."

6. *Coffee or a cold shower will sober you up.* People will believe anything in the perpetual search for something that will ease the pain of a hangover and at the same time have a sobering effect.

The *fact* is that the old joke still stands: A cold shower will make you a wet drunk; a cup of coffee will make you a wide-awake drunk. Time alone will sober you up. It takes about an hour for the effect of each drink to wear off. So if you've had more than enough, sleep it off or don't drink too much in the first place.

7. *Alcoholic people can learn to drink socially.* This is potentially the most life-threatening myth. It is held by many people,

particularly those who want to believe it so that they may continue their own drinking.

The *fact* is that so few alcoholics can safely drink socially that it makes absolutely no sense for those vulnerable people to try it.

8. *All alcoholics are weak-willed, immoral people who lack self-discipline and the ability to differentiate right from wrong.* This view of the alcoholic person is a direct outgrowth of the prohibitionist movement. Since alcoholism has been established by the American Medical Association as an illness, the myth is beginning to dissipate.

The *fact* is that alcoholism is an addiction. Some people recover spontaneously; a large portion of the remainder respond to treatment, without regard to the nature of their character.

9. *Alcoholism is a self-inflicted illness.* The prohibitionist movement also encouraged the view that since alcoholism is self-inflicted getting well requires only the cessation of the act of lifting the glass (or bottle) to the lip. Anyone can do it. Would that it were that simple.

The *fact* is, as Dr. Sheila Blume, former director of the New York State Division of Alcoholism and former medical director of the National Council on Alcoholism, points out: "The fact that an alcoholic patient must take a great deal of responsibility for his/her recovery is also common to other chronic diseases where responsibility for following a regimen of diet, medication, therapy, exercise, etc., lies with the patient. This does not mean the illness was self-induced."

10. *Most alcoholics are men; women rarely become addicted.*

The *fact* is that at one time there were about four times as many known male alcoholics as female. However, the gap may not have been as great as it appeared because women were traditionally at home and therefore more able to hide their drinking. As women come into the workforce and compete in the male business world, they join the groups of lunchtime drinkers and overstressed competitors. No one really knows if the number of women alcoholics is increasing, but women certainly seem to be edging their way toward equality with men.

There are additional myths that are not so widespread or so potentially dangerous, but they remain myths. For example:

- It is impolite to refuse a drink.
- Alcohol gives you energy.
- A party without alcohol is a flop.
- Mixing drinks will make a person drunker.

As you dispel these myths about alcohol and alcoholism, the facts will surface. Then, as you teach them to your children, they will be able to reject the misinformation that passes for the truth among their peers.

What do your children need to know? They need to know that alcohol is a drug; that it is a drug that affects different people in different ways; that alcohol is absorbed rapidly into the bloodstream and goes directly to the brain, where it impairs judgment, slows down reaction time, and dulls the senses. They need to know that alcohol is addictive and, as children or grandchildren of at least one alcoholic, they are at risk of developing drinking problems themselves. And they need to know that there is help for people who develop the disease of alcoholism and that the earlier it is treated the more hope there is for lasting recovery. Those are the simple facts; they need to be repeated and discussed until they become firmly woven into the belief system of your children.

Your Children's Drinking

Adult children of alcoholics often ask what else they as parents can do so their children won't get into difficulties with alcohol. The thing to remember is that you are the model for your children's behavior. This cuts right to the core of what responsible parenting is all about. To help define that model, consider the findings of researchers who have studied the characteristics of families that have avoided the alcohol trap.

In these families, drinking is always part of other activities such as a meal or a religious celebration. Drunkenness is unacceptable, and so is any heavy drinking. Alcohol is not seen or used as a painkiller, an indication of manhood, or an acceptable sedative. It is neither a panacea nor a curse. No one is pressured into drinking; nor is drinking condemned as evil. Attitudes are generally neutral. The parents themselves set an example of moderation in their drinking and in their lives, and avoid lecturing their children. Rules about drinking or not drinking are clear-cut and understood by all. Children in these families are gradually introduced to alcohol long before the legal drinking age. (You may want to look at this item carefully because of the emotional impact it can have in your family.) Families who don't drink don't scorn those who do or hold them up as horrible examples.

Keeping these precepts in mind, there are things you can do to build a good family model. You can talk to your children about the power of peer pressure. You can let them know you understand by sharing examples from your own life. One man acknowledges that he hates wearing jeans. They itch and they're stiff. "But everybody wears them, so I do too."

A touchy topic for young people is parties—who serves what, wears what, plays what, does what. Most people love to talk about parties, both those they've been to and those that are being planned. And it is at parties that peer pressure can be excruciating. If you can talk with your children about their parties, your parties, and those you have together, and can do so in a way that puts the emphasis on fun, you will probably succeed in keeping lines of communication open. Tell them about your own adolescence and what you did when you were their age. If you feel critical of or threatened by the kinds of parties your children are having, you'll only make them go into hiding if you talk to them in negative terms. Instead, try to remember that they are going through the same stages you went through and that you too deeply wished that your parents had understood you.

Try to understand their music, clothing, speech, and so on, rather than criticizing it. You undoubtedly can remember when your adolescent crowd had its particular passing fancy, whether it was Peter Pan collars, Hula-Hoops, or the Grateful Dead. Even if you understand their fads you don't have to subscribe to them, but you certainly can see where they're coming from and lend an interested ear.

Another practical thing you can do is to assign adult responsibilities that will give them a sense of your respect. Many kids say they drink because it makes them feel grown up. If you can offer alternative ways for them to feel mature, they may be intrigued and not resort to drinking. One family helped their children open a small bank account and allowed them to keep the bankbooks, make deposits and withdrawals, and keep track of their own "cash flow." Another family kept a junked car in the backyard. The thirteen-year-old twins spent all their spare time there; they pretended they were on the racetrack and made all the appropriate noises, jumping in and out to "rev up" and fix the engine.

Baby-sitting for younger siblings or neighborhood children is also a good way for young people to gain a sense of being needed and being responsible. Needless to say, any activity you suggest to them has to be appropriate for their age and in keeping with your children's ability and interests.

Finally, a few attitudes you may not even be aware of can have serious implications as your children grow up and therefore need to be watched carefully. For example, you may praise the alcohol tolerance of those who have "hollow legs" or can "drink anyone under the table." This is not a virtue, but an ominous sign of danger. Or you may offer imitation cocktails such as Shirley Temples (orange juice with a shot of lime and a cherry stuck on the rim of the glass). This just glamorizes drinking and is really unnecessary, particularly for children who have alcoholism in their families. Nonalcoholic beverages can be just as enticing when called plain old orange juice.

You may express a need for a drink when you feel tired, dismayed, or anxious. It is an all too common experience for a child to observe a parent come home from work and say, before he or she closes the front door, "I had a lousy day. I've got to have a drink." Or you may tend to push drinks on friends or visitors. The message then gets across to your children that socializing must include drinking. You may also overstock your refrigerator with beer and mixers or you may have a bar out in the open with liquor always easily available. Again, your children will interpret this to mean "every warm, hospitable household must have an ample supply of drinks on hand." If you're feeling overwhelmed by things you've never considered before, relax. As you can see, there is a lot parents can do to help their children avoid the hidden dangers.

Your Children and Your Parents

What should you tell your children about your parents' drinking if it is still going on? The most important thing is to tell the truth and not pussyfoot around even though you may feel ill at ease. Don't avoid reality by telling your child that your mother is weaving around because she has a problem with her balance or your father always smells that way because his teeth are loose. But make sure that what you do tell a child is geared to that child's age and ability to understand what is going on.

When a three-year-old asks why grandpa smells so funny, you might tell him that your father has been drinking beer and explain that people smell like what they have been eating or drinking. "You smell like candy after you've had a piece of chocolate," for instance. It will be hard for a young child to understand much more. If the child notices erratic behavior, go one step further and point out that people who drink sometimes act in ways that are difficult to explain. You might add that people act differently on different days, according to how they feel, just as your child sometimes acts like a grouch when he or she is sick.

A seven-year-old will need a more sophisticated explanation. At this point the drinking can be described in terms of an illness. Help your child understand that a powerful drug, alcohol, acts on the brain to produce behavior that is difficult to understand.

Older children, adolescents in particular, will need to know still more. There's no sense rehashing horror stories of what happened in your past. But teenagers can be helped to understand that angry feelings in the family sometimes interfere with closeness and communication. Stress the fact that the person who is drinking too much is ill and that some of the mean things that person does are not purposeful or directed specifically at anyone else. Steer clear of judgments or diagnoses. Only an expert can say a person is or is not an alcoholic.

It's important to remember that your children's reactions to your parents may not be the same as yours. One daughter of an alcoholic mother was surprised to find that *her* daughters had a close friendship with their grandmother even though she continued to drink. For the brief periods she was with them, she could give them the devoted attention she had never been able to focus on her own children.

If you have forbidden your drinking parent to drive with your children in the car, you will have to let the children know that driving and drinking don't mix and that their safety is your responsibility. But you can also tell them that when their grandparent gets better and stops drinking they will be able to spend time to-gether. One woman ran out of the house when she saw her father come weaving into the driveway in his car. "Get out of here and don't come back," she screamed. If your children do witness an incident like this, you will again have to discuss in plain terms how alcohol affects the brain.

You may be uneasy about what your children say to neighbors or friends about drinking or drunkenness. You may have taught them that certain things are not talked about outside the house, and that every family has some things that are private. This rule may work for daddy's income or sister's breakup with her boy-friend. But in the case of drinking, you may just have to let them talk. Telling them not to say anything will only reinforce the fam-ily secret for another generation.

8

You and
Your Parents Now

Children begin by loving their parents; as they
grow older they judge them; sometimes they forgive them.

Oscar Wilde, *The Picture of Dorian Gray*

Growing up in an alcoholic home can be so bewildering that
you may still not be certain alcohol was behind the turmoil.
John W. Jones, Ph.D., developed a set of thirty questions,
called the C.A.S.T. (Children of Alcoholics Screening Test) test, as
a way of identifying children of alcoholics in hospital-based treatment centers. Five of these questions appear below. If you answer
yes to even one, you can be sure that one of your parents was
drinking too much.

1. Have you ever thought that one of your parents had a
   drinking problem?

2. Did you ever argue or fight with a parent when he or she
   was drinking?

3. Did you ever wish that a parent would stop drinking?

4. Did you ever feel responsible for or guilty about a parent's
   drinking?

5. Have you ever felt sick, cried, or had a "knot" in your stomach after worrying about a parent's drinking?

Maybe the drinking has stopped by now. Maybe it is still going on. Maybe it began only recently and is a new problem. Or maybe your alcoholic parent has died and you are having a tough time with the surviving spouse. No matter what is going on, the drinking must have affected your life, the life of your parents, and your relationship with them. Only when you understand and face the aftermath of the drinking will you be able to distinguish between the havoc that was created by alcoholism and the difficulties that arise as part of everyday living. Then you can go on to realistic plans for making things different.

Guilt Trips

"Every time I wake up in the morning I feel riddled with guilt. I don't need anyone else to put me down." Every alcoholic feels guilt about his or her drinking. The problem is that guilt is not a good motivator for change. It is too easily rationalized, denied, or drowned in alcohol. It has a self-perpetuating quality that serves only to slide the drinker deeper into what the Reverend Jody Kellerman labels "a merry-go-round called denial" and then heaps guilt upon guilt. So if you are trying to establish a constructive relationship with your alcoholic parent, you can be most helpful by working to alleviate the guilt rather than by punishing your parent further. Pointing out the destructive qualities and outcomes of the drinking will be helpful only if it is done with minimal emotional overtones and an emphasis on facts.

For example, Alice, a recovering alcoholic, remembers how her husband helped her realize that she had to do something about her drinking. "He gave me the silent treatment. It was more of a cool statement than an emotion. 'You ruined the dinner again,' he would say. It was stated as a simple fact and I couldn't argue or fight back or get rid of the guilt that was in me because he had left me no room to deny or yell back. There was the burned dinner on top of the stove the next morning."

One of the most effective intervention procedures is based on just this process—letting the alcoholic know the consequences of the drinking without pointing fingers. Attention shifts away from the alcoholic and focuses on friends and family, who learn to distinguish between behaviors that are caused by the drinking and behaviors that are targeted deliberately at family members to unnerve them. A description of how to implement an effective "intervention" appears in Vernon Johnson's book *I'll Quit Tomorrow*. If your parent is still drinking, get hold of a copy! In it you will learn how to gather family, friends, co-workers, and other concerned people together in order to let the alcoholic know how the drinking is affecting each one. Such a meeting must be done from a loving, understanding stance and must be carefully rehearsed, usually in conjunction with a professional alcoholism counselor. It should always include plans for referral for treatment if and when the alcoholic comes to the point of recognizing the problem and accepting help.

It is important to remember that *denial* is one of the primary symptoms of alcoholism. It is perpetuated much longer by the alcoholic than by those around him, for it serves a crucial purpose—to block out the unfaceable pain. The alcoholic uses it to protect himself and holds on to it tenaciously in the face of tremendous opposition and contradictory evidence.

Some alcoholics land in treatment facilities before they themselves acknowledge that there is a drinking problem. They agree to be admitted only to placate their families or to avoid losing a job. Dr. LeClair Bissell, former director of the Smithers Treatment Center in New York, once said ironically of the patients in her alcoholism unit, "We don't admit alcoholics here. They are all wrongfully accused. We have exactly four weeks to turn them into alcoholics."

Preparations need to be made in advance in case there is a possibility that the alcoholic will accept a referral plan. Finding the right place can be a complicated matchmaking process that requires taking into account geographical considerations, financial arrangements, special needs of the alcoholic, previous treatment experiences (both positive and negative), availability of medical help, availability of Alcoholics Anonymous, and so on. It is foolhardy to risk having an alcoholic change his mind while referral procedures and details are being worked out. And don't think for a minute that a crafty alcoholic wouldn't take advantage of a delay to change the entire course of events.

Talking to Friends

What should you tell friends about your parent's alcoholism? Some of them will know all about it before you say anything. What you tell others will depend on how close you feel to them and whether it is pertinent or expedient to tell them. If you are looking for comfort or reassurance about a specific incident, you will probably want to let good friends know the total picture.

It will be easier to talk about your parent's alcoholism with friends who understand drinking problems, particularly if they themselves are recovering alcoholics or children of alcoholics. If they are not, you could take it upon yourself to discuss alcoholism with them (the best way to learn about anything is to teach it). If your parent is recovering, you may need to preserve anonymity until you have been given permission to talk.

Generally it is not wise to spread the news that someone is drinking too much. Privacy has to be respected. The news will get around by itself, for an active alcoholic is usually his own best advertisement. However, you should not feel forced to cover up. You can confirm the observations of others without making accusations.

This is how Margaret handled the situation. One of her mother's bridge friends called her to complain that the game was falling apart because Margaret's mother drank heavily during the weekly gatherings and could hardly see her own cards much of the time. The call came after Margaret's mother had spilled her drink across the bridge table and onto her partner's expensive skirt. "Does your mother drink that much all the time?" asked her bridge partner. Margaret answered with a question: "Is that what you saw?"

"Yes. I think you should talk to your mom about her drinking. We're all worried about her, but we don't think it's our place to say anything. We're afraid the game is going to fall apart and, as you know, we've been playing for six years."

"Well," said Margaret, "it's up to you to choose whom you play bridge with. I don't want to get into something that is really between you folks and mom. If playing bridge is impossible, you can still be friends. I don't know about mom, but I've read about people with drinking problems. They seem to need their friends."

Perhaps Margaret was wisely, maybe even unconsciously, setting the stage for a future intervention using Vernon Johnson's technique. She was not going to talk about her mother's drinking; she would neither deny it nor confirm it. But the observations of these bridge-playing friends might someday help propel her mother into treatment.

A Family Assistance Program

Employee assistance programs, sometimes called employee alcoholism programs, have been tremendously successful in reducing the incidence of employee accidents, absenteeism, tardiness, and errors due to alcoholism. Success rates range between 60 percent and 80 percent. These programs are relatively simple: A policy is developed and distributed companywide to employees. Supervisors are instructed on how to implement it. They are not to make diagnoses but are to refer troubled employees to either an in-house company health service or a designated outside counselor to try to pinpoint the problem. If there is a drinking problem, employees are told that they must do something about it because their jobs are in jeopardy. They are given several chances to make a change, but if work-related incidents continue they may lose their jobs. Company executives have learned that employees generally are more interested in keeping their jobs than their families, their health, or their social standing. And they will often go for help when the pressure is on at work.

The industrial program model has been adapted for use with high school students who are having trouble with alcohol and/or other drugs. Known as the student assistance program, it has been implemented under the direction of Ellen Morehouse, a social worker, in a number of high schools in Westchester County, New York. At the outset of the program, a clear-cut policy is shared with all school personnel, parents, and students so that no misunderstandings arise about what behaviors lead to what consequences.

Although a family's own "assistance program" cannot be exactly like an industrial or school one, it too can involve a clear statement of intention related to stated goals. Just as the employee knows the consequences of drinking on job security and the student knows the consequences of drinking in school, so the alcoholic parent can be told the consequences of drinking as they relate to his or her family. Family members can establish a prede-termined course *in writing,* to be followed when certain situations arise. The policy does away with ambiguity and allows people to act with conviction.

The effectiveness of such a contract will depend on whether the family can come to a realistic consensus and the strength of each member's commitment to carrying out policy issues as they are written. The contract should be composed with the thought that later changes can be made, but at least for the time being the items are indisputable and available for reference.

Since the policy is to be agreed upon by the whole family, the alcoholic should be included in the planning. Discussion should take place when the alcoholic is sober so he can fully understand the content. In some situations a policy will have to be formulated by the family and presented to the alcoholic as a fait accompli, but even then it should be shared when the alcoholic can best absorb its meaning.

Such a policy can be upsetting to the alcoholic, particularly if he has not yet recognized the impact of his drinking on family life. He needs to be told that things have been confusing for much of the family and that its members are now attempting to straighten out certain persistent problems. The matter needs to be handled in a kind, nonpunitive way, but a way that sounds like the family means what it says.

In addition to the alcoholic and immediate family members, grandchildren should be included in any planning and policy if they are old enough and able to understand. They will feel more able to cope and won't be left adrift guessing what's wrong and why people are doing what they are doing.

Some families will want to have the policy signed by everyone so that it becomes more like an official document. That, of course, will be each family's choice. In any case, a written policy will keep you from having to make important decisions suddenly. Also, your responses will be backed by others. You will not have made them in a vacuum. The unexpected or surprise element will be taken out of decision making. Then the alcoholic as well as others involved will benefit by clear, decisive actions taken in response to specific occurrences. As the drinker becomes aware of the consequences of the drinking, the stage may be set for further action.

Developing a Family Policy

When someone is still drinking too much, how do you develop a family policy in terms of what's going on and what to do about it? You may find that your family cannot agree about what is happening. You must begin by getting the stories straight.

One woman describes her family this way: Her adult brother, age thirty-eight, still lives with his alcoholic mother and protects her from the consequences of her drinking. This woman is continually frustrated because her brother does not see the situation in the same way. For example, after she receives a disjointed midnight phone call from her drunken mother, her brother will get on the phone and say, "Hi there, how's everything?" He never acknowledges the mother's condition or why the call was made in the first place. He goes on as if nothing were happening, and garbled midnight calls have become a customary part of everyone's life. He doesn't listen to his sister when she tries to question him or talk to him about their mother's behavior, which seems bizarre to her but is ignored by him. Not only does she feel bewildered, but she has begun to question her own perception of the situation and to doubt her own view of reality. What is and what is not has been a problem for her since she was young. For her and others like her, there are five steps that go into forming a family policy.

I. *Defining the Boundaries of Reality*

Fuzzy boundaries are perpetuated each time something happens that is viewed one way by one family member and another way by someone else. Some families are able to figure it all out, but usually not without the help of a nonpartisan professional or family friend. In the case described above, it took several years of therapy before brother and sister came to realize that they had to join together to arrive at an objective reality. When they finally understood that their mother was pitting one against the other in order to take the focus off herself, they were able to make changes. After a catastrophic family dinner (everything burned) the two young people left the house, went out together to the movies, and afterward began seriously to discuss what to do. Ultimately the brother moved out of his mother's house and she, faced with unbearable loneliness, checked herself into an alcoholism rehabilitation unit.

II. *Defining Goals*

Goals must be set before policies and plans can be implemented. Goals are:

1. To help the entire family do away with denial of the problem.

2. To promote mutual understanding among family members.

3. To allow family members to act from a considered agreement.

4. To relieve individuals from coming to decisions alone and thus making them more comfortable with choices.

5. To help the alcoholic make changes that may lead to an end to the drinking.

III. *Creating Specific Policies*

Policies must be understandable and agreed to by each family member. "Family members" in this case include the extended family and all close or caring people, particularly those who are living with or who come into daily contact with the afflicted person. This step should include concrete ways of dealing with such situations as baby-sitting, driving, visiting, holidays, making phone calls, speaking to your friends and your parents' friends, keeping alcohol available in your home and your parents' home, and so on. Here is a suggested inventory that covers a wide range of potential conflicts around which policies can be formed:

- **Basics**

    Money and finances
    > If you live with your parents, who will pay for what? Will you lend money to your parents? Will you borrow from them? If your parents drink up their pension or Social Security income, will you come to the rescue?

    Living arrangements
    > What are the conditions under which you might live together? If you know you cannot live with your parents, how can you be both kind and firm about your decision?

Health provisions

Will you pay for your parents' medical care? To what extent? Will you permit smoking/drinking in your household? Will you permit the use of other drugs in your household? Will you help with transportation to and from medical care or medical facilities?

Friends and relatives

Will you keep the "family secret," or will you let your relatives and parents' friends in on it?

• Holidays

Where should celebrations take place?
At your home?
At your parents' home?
On neutral territory?
How many guests should be invited? What should be served?
What constitutes a suitable gift for a given occasion?

• Telephone calls

What are appropriate times for telephone calls?
How can calls be terminated?
Should collect calls be accepted?
What are topics that are suitable subjects for telephone conversations?

• Visits

Where will you and your parents visit one another?
How long should any one visit be?
What are the reasons for terminating a visit?

• Grandchildren

Will you allow your parents to baby-sit? At your home or theirs?
Under what circumstances and for how long?
Will you allow your parents to take care of your children on trips, in cars, at movies?

• **Liquor**

> Is liquor kept in your home?
> Who supplies it or buys it?
> When is drinking appropriate?
> Should there be no drinking in your family?

You don't need a lawyer to draw up a family agreement. It can be as simple as the one shown below.

SAMPLE FAMILY AGREEMENT

Parents: Mary D. Jones, Bill Jones
Children: Peter Jones, Rhonda J. Smith, Stuart Jones
Others: Robert Smith (brother-in-law); Alice D. Johnson (mother's sister); Albert Johnson (mother's brother-in-law); Robert Smith, Jr. (grandchild)

1. We do not pretend that no one knows about the drinking. Everyone knows, and we know everyone knows.

2. We will make no excuses to those in authority—courts, police, and others.

3. We will never make excuses to bosses about absenteeism, tardiness, errors, or other alcohol-related problems.

4. If we detect that our parent has been drinking, we will not speak to that parent on the phone.

5. We will not change our drinking habits just because our parents are around.

6. We will never buy alcoholic beverages for our parent.

7. We will not clean or fix up messes that are consequences of too much drinking. ("Messes" include broken furniture, banged-up cars, spilled food or drink, burns.)

8. We will not drive in any kind of vehicle nor will we allow our children to drive with anyone who has had so much as one drink.

9. We will not allow any child care or baby-sitting, day or night, unless our parent has not been drinking for at least two years.

10. We will remain "cool" about complaints about each other, friends,

or neighbors, and about hangovers and other health matters related to drinking. We will not get involved in discussions about financial needs and alcohol-related accidents or fights.

We agree that the above statement is fair and reasonable and further agree to follow its terms and conditions.

Signatures of all those named above:

_____   _____

_____   _____

A copy should be made for each family member or the original should be placed in an accessible spot (for example, on the front of the refrigerator or on a bulletin board) so that it can be referred to easily.

A family policy may lessen the element of spontaneity within the family because people are aware of rules that dictate behavior. But sometimes spontaneity has to be sacrificed in order to reduce chaos. Also, a policy can be firm but still have flexibility built into it so that as things progress parts of it can be scrapped or replaced. For instance, one couple decided to let their children drive with their grandfather only if he had not been drinking. When they opened the trunk one Sunday to put the baby's stroller in it, they discovered a bottle of Scotch hidden there. Now the rule has changed—there is no driving with the children until the grandfather has not had a drink for at least a year—and this amendment has been agreed on as family policy.

IV. *Making Alternative Plans*
Because the alcoholic is an unpredictable person and new ways of coping must be found, you will need to be open to the possibility of making changes. An example is the family who agreed not to talk to their father on the phone if he was drinking. As it turned out, however, not all family members were equally sensitive to his state of inebriation as they spoke on the phone. And they did not want to have a misunderstanding with him that might lead to cutting him off if, in fact, he had not been drinking. So they decided

that, if possible, a second person should get on the line at every call—to "validate" (on the extension) the perception of the other.

V. *Maintaining Continuing Communications*

Family members must know what is happening and how each one is dealing with specific situations as they arise or change.

A policy is only as effective as people's resolve to stick with it and mean what they have said. When people back down or make exceptions, the efficacy of a family policy is jeopardized. Family members who separate themselves from what is going on should be challenged. One young man said that as he tried to deal with his father's drinking his brother became more and more distant and came up with all kinds of rationalizations for not wanting to have anything to do with the entire matter. He said he was too busy; he said he had been too hurt; he said his brother would be listened to and he would not; he said he thought God would take care of their father and he certainly didn't want to interfere.

Finally, this young man told his brother that he *needed* his help, that he could not contend with their father alone, and that if they did not act as a team there would be more and more difficulty for both of them. Eventually his brother acquiesced and joined him in helping the father recover.

Of course, it takes a strong family to be able to work together to create a pact and stick to it—and by definition families of alcoholics are often in serious trouble and have a long way to go before they can trust one another enough to work toward a common goal. They often have such a long history of quarrels, competition, and hurt and feel so immensely threatened by each other that they try to go it alone.

A Contract with Yourself

Jean is the daughter of an alcoholic in one such family, the middle child of three girls. She describes herself as having come "unhinged" and she has gone to a psychiatrist for help. In the course of her therapy, her doctor suggested that she bring one of her sisters to a session or two so that he could more fully understand the family dynamics and be more helpful to his patient. However, neither of the sisters would go with her. They both agreed that Jean was the sick one and they didn't need a doctor.

Jean is seen as the family villain because she sees less of their alcoholic mother, who keeps the other daughters involved with her every day even though they have their own families. They are afraid to antagonize her by pulling away from the nest, which is seething with intrigue and complicated relationships. Jean describes her childhood as so full of noise and confusion that no one noticed or had to deal with the drinking. "Chaos was used as a cover-up," she explains. Apparently every member of the family was able to create so much confusion that no one had to get in touch with feelings—and the family still manages to keep things that way.

If your family will never be able to work together, you should consider seeking help from the community—from mental health professionals, clergy, or friends. Or you may want to consider making a contract with yourself. This is what Jean did. The contract gave her an opportunity to think things out clearly in advance and to avoid making complicated decisions while under pressure. The contract is explicit in its suggestions on what to do in many situations. For instance, when her mother falls in her plate at dinner, Jean now knows that she has permission from herself to get up from the table and leave. She has also given herself permission not to listen to her mother's critical tirades. She leaves the room, hangs up the phone, turns up the volume on the television, goes back to her book, or puts her hands over her ears. This last response infuriates her mother, but she sometimes does it anyhow. She only knows that it preserves her sanity, and it is written in the contract she has made with herself.

In making a contract with yourself, you may find the categories outlined on pages 115–17 useful. Some may not be applicable, or you may want to add some of your own. It's difficult to imagine all the things that could possibly happen, particularly when you are dealing with a person who is drinking too much. What could possibly go wrong—or right? Two examples:

"The doctor told my dad to stop drinking—and he did!"

"I thought my mother was all set in the nursing home when they found the empties in her closet. And out she went!"

You probably will be able to use most of the categories listed. It's helpful to remember the motto used by the American Field Service in training students who will be placed in foreign countries: "Expect the unexpected."

If Your Parent Is No Longer Drinking

Is there any point in dwelling on the past or trying to punish either of your parents for their inadequacies? What has happened has happened and there is no changing it now. Whether you want to go over the injustices of the past will depend on various factors. First of all, you will have to be conscious of the fact that it will engender a lot of guilt and pain. But you might feel that it is worth doing if it clarifies matters for you and helps you understand what went on. It will be easiest if you bring the matter up in the course of casual conversation.

It took courage and a dozen years for two brothers to clear up the following mystery by finally asking, "Why did you do it?" When they were nine and ten years old, the brothers stayed with their aunt for about a year. Their beds were moved suddenly to the aunt's house and they concluded that their parents had abandoned them permanently. That they were abruptly switched from one household to another was not so awful, but why they had been abandoned was never explained. No one would be definite about when their parents would return or where they had gone, and no logical explanations were given for the move. When they returned to their own home, no one said anything about why they had been deserted and they were afraid to ask questions. In fact, they were told not to ask—that someday they would understand. But for many years they never understood.

As it turned out, their aunt had taken them in because both parents were drinking heavily and could not manage the household and the children. It was at the parents' request that the boys had been moved. When things were finally explained, they saw that the move had been made out of humanitarian concern and not out of malice. In looking back, they were grateful. But leaving two young children in the dark for so long was nothing short of cruelty. When things go unsaid, misunderstandings are bred.

Sometimes explanations come when the drinking stops. At that point, the situation may have improved enough for questions to be asked. But a lot still goes on after the drinking has ended, and there are sure to be many residual problems related to the alcoholism or the strains of staying sober. Family members have to remember that sobriety through abstinence is a matter of life and death for the alcoholic, and to question the procedure can only be harmful. Accept your parent's selection of a means to stay sober and rejoice in it, even if you have to put up with what may appear to be mysterious choices. Your alcoholic parent, for instance, may choose to attend an AA meeting rather than your birthday celebration. It would certainly show sensitivity and consideration on your part if you arranged the party for another day or at another time so that it did not conflict with the AA meeting, which must be *first* on any alcoholic's list of priorities.

Dealing with the newly sober person is very different from dealing with one who hasn't had a drink for years. In recognizing this, you can adjust your expectations and know that as the sober period increases there will be positive personality changes and more flexibility. Your alcoholic parent will be able to act more rationally as he or she copes with stress and discomfort without resorting to the bottle.

A slip back into drinking after a period of time without alcohol is one of the most painful episodes to experience. For the grownup child of an alcoholic, it may seem like the world is going to crash in again, as it did in childhood. But, as Dr. Terence Wilson of Rutgers University points out, a slip is a mistake, not a failure. It is almost inevitable in the long, hard fight against alcoholism and should not be used to make your parent feel guilty or discouraged. Recovery may be closer than it seems.

No recently recovered alcoholic wants to be confronted immediately with compliments about the fact that he or she has stopped drinking. The subject is a touchy one at best. However, alcoholics may very well enjoy being told that they are looking better—and then *they* can tell *you* the reason. If you have been in on the recovery period from the beginning, it may be helpful to give your parent this kind of affirmation.

At the same time, you need to remember that only the alcoholic is in charge of maintaining sobriety. It is not your responsibility, just as the drinking was not your responsibility. It is not up to you to empty bottles containing alcoholic beverages, nor is it appropriate now for you to suggest if, how, or where liquor should be stored in your parents' home.

At dinner in a restaurant one night a man offered his father, who was sober in AA, a sip of his rum punch. This "friendly" gesture was probably the most hostile act imaginable. Every family contract should include a policy on offering —or not offering—alcoholic beverages at home. And it is only common sense to know that neither you nor any member of your family should give alcoholic beverages as gifts.

If your parent is sober in AA, you can learn more about the program if you go to an open AA meeting. Your parent may be glad to have you go along, but if he or she would rather you go to some other meeting, respect that decision and find an AA group elsewhere. You will certainly be welcome at an open meeting, and you will learn exactly what the process is that keeps people sober—one day at a time.

If your parent stops drinking, it will be helpful for you to understand how he or she does it and what you can do (or not do) in order to help ensure continuing abstinence. If your parent invites you to a session with his or her therapist, accept the invitation. This may be an extraordinary opportunity to learn more about your parent, about alcoholism, and about how the illness has affected the interactions within your family over the years.

Sometimes the reality that a parent has stopped drinking and is managing life well doesn't seem to sink in. Doreen still acts as if her mother, who stopped drinking eight years ago, will set the house on fire with her careless smoking. Although she now lives away from home, she finds herself leaving work in a panic and stopping at her parents' house to check on them. She is haunted by fears, all connected to what was happening when her mother was not only drinking but drunk a lot of the time. Doreen still cannot shake off the need to reassure herself about her parents' well-being, although they now need no caretaking and probably don't appreciate her unannounced arrivals.

Time takes care of some scars, but the more deep-seated ones will go away only when they are understood and worked through in therapy, or religious experience, or by achieving some new understanding of the past. It is likely that a part of this understanding will come through the acceptance of the concept of alcoholism as a disease. But even then you may still be perplexed and may still have difficulties. These will reverse themselves only when you come to understand their origins and learn to cope with them in terms that are appropriate to your life now.

Getting Together

If the relationship between you and your drinking parent has deteriorated so much that you do not spend any time with each other, you may want to try to find workable ways of being together. It *is* possible. One man said about his alcoholic mother, "I'd given up on her. She wasn't going to change and I didn't want to waste my energy trying to change her." But two years later this young man's relationship with his mother and his attitude toward her had altered completely. Even though she was still drinking, his despair had vanished. What caused the turnabout? In this case it was the faith and devotion of another son, who kept in daily touch with his mother. He finally persuaded all eight of his brothers and sisters that if they encouraged her and worked together, talking and listening to her, she could get well. She, in turn, talked about her own fears and stopped blaming her children for what had happened. As his sisters and brothers began to be more open with each other, the man who had kept away found it easier to visit his mother occasionally and see for himself that the situation was not hopeless. Now he is full of confidence that something will trigger a change and she will recover.

In some families, though, staying away seems to work best. Sometimes the only contacts are on the phone and then usually when the alcoholic is drunk or drinking. One man says that if his father calls him when he is drunk and rambling he says, "Dad, let's talk in the morning. I don't understand you now." And he hangs up. He feels this is the only truly humane way to deal with an impossible drinking parent.

An alcoholism counselor whose mother is alcoholic has worked out another way of keeping in touch without becoming too involved. "It used to be I'd get a postcard from my parents and feel like killing myself," he says. "Then I didn't have any contact with them for four years. Finally, I wrote to them and said, 'If you want any kind of relationship with me, never put me down again.' Now we talk on the telephone, but we don't visit. I don't believe you have to work everything out. Sometimes," he adds, "a divorce is appropriate."

After an Alcoholic Parent Has Died

Sometimes it is death rather than a conscious decision that breaks the involvement with an alcoholic parent. If you now have a single nonalcoholic parent, you may want to form a completely new and more understanding relationship with him or her.

You will probably benefit by reminiscing with your mother or father about happy times, funny times, stressful times, and frightening times. Some of the events you remember will be sad for you both. However, talking over what happened may bring buried feelings to the surface where they will have a chance to lose their haunting aspect and some of their emotional charge. You and your parent can also focus on present activities that you can now enjoy together—walking, shopping, travel, books, televison, current fads and fashions, your children (if you have them), relatives, health concerns, social events, a birthday party, a picnic, and so on.

A young businessman whose alcoholic mother died five years ago invites his father, who lives 3,000 miles away, to stay with him for several months each fall. Together they have laid a brick path to the house, replaced much of the old house's wiring, built a bunk bed for one of the grandsons, erected a basketball hoop, and completed many other housekeeping jobs that had always been put off before. Father and son needed each other for these projects and their respect grew as they worked together. The mother's drinking had kept them apart for many years, for she demanded all her husband's attention and in not so subtle ways had kept them from enjoying a natural closeness.

Maybe your widowed mother or father has remarried, introducing a completely new person to the scene. It is common for the widow of an alcoholic to marry another alcoholic. If that has happened in your family, take a deep breath and get to work on a new family policy. Do it slowly, because you are dealing with an unfamiliar constellation of factors that are delicate for all concerned. Self-blame, guilt, and the new family dynamics will need addressing. You will probably want to talk together as openly as possible, respecting one another's sensibilities.

When the Alcoholism Is New, the Parent Old

After a lifetime of normal drinking, a growing number of people over sixty or sixty-five begin to use alcohol in ways that can lead to trouble. Perhaps they feel cut off and fearful. Most have suffered serious losses—a family member, a job, health, home, status, friends, income, or freedom. "For men," points out Dr. Edith Gomberg of the University of Michigan School of Social Work, who has studied this problem, "retirement or loss of spouse are most stressful." Whatever the loss, some people begin to use more and more alcohol to lessen the sad feelings or temporarily get rid of them. Unwittingly, they develop tolerance for the drug and then get hooked on it. Older people, perhaps because of metabolic or other changes, seem to become addicted more readily than middle-aged people.

Many older people become affected because their physicians prescribe alcohol for relief of anxiety or to induce sleep. They feel easier about taking alcohol when it is for "medicinal purposes." A talk with your parent's doctor may call attention to the potential hazards of such a prescription. Also, it is dangerous to combine alcohol with other medications, particularly sedatives or sleeping pills (Dalmane, Doriden, Noctec), which depress the central nervous system. Since alcohol too is a depressant, this is adding a downer to a downer, and there can be an unexpected reaction. Enough of both or either can cause death. Most older people are taking some pill for some ailment, so alcohol and drug interactions have to be carefully monitored.

Sorting Out Symptoms

If your parent has become dependent on alcohol later in life, your chances of helping the parent do something about it are much greater than they would be if the problem had begun earlier. First of all, you're now in a more powerful position—an adult, not a child. Second, there are signs you can look for in order to identify the problem early—hidden bottles; smell of alcohol on the breath early in the day; slurred speech; impaired balance; denial of necessity to drink; thinly veiled excuses for drinking at inappropriate times; physical problems, particularly those related to withdrawal (such as the "shakes"); unexplained bruises and burns; falls and forgetfulness; and periods of erratic thinking.

Of course, the trick here is to sort out the symptoms of oncoming old age from those of alcoholism. They are very similar and you will need to be careful before you come to a firm conclusion or a diagnosis. Other relatives or people who are in close contact with your parent may be able to help.

"I had never noticed it, but my mother claimed she had always been shaky in the morning. She had me completely fooled," a woman says. "She would sneak a drink at noon after assuring me that the shaking would automatically stop as the day progressed. I didn't give her an argument until one day I smelled the 'stuff' on her breath. Then I knew where the shakes had come from. Shakes that stop with a drink are not signs of aging, they are signs of drinking!"

But there is the other side of the coin. "My father lived alone. I worried about him because he began to be forgetful and could hardly remember anything, including where he had put his shoes, his eyeglasses, his wallet, and so on. Then it seemed he couldn't count change, missed appointments, and was vague about many matters that he had previously taken care of. He had been a one-cocktail man all his life and sometimes had a beer or two on weekend afternoons. But now that he lived alone, after my mom's death, we suspected that he had begun to drink too much. As it turned out, we were completely wrong. He was developing early symptoms of Alzheimer's disease—drinking was not the problem at all."

People often say, "Why bother about alcoholism late in life? Why not let the drinker enjoy his favorite drink. He doesn't have that much longer to live anyway." But alcoholism is a terrible and painful disease at any age and should not be ignored. As with many other illnesses, the earlier a problem is identified, the more hope there is for recovery. And older people will need to know the facts, will need to come to realize what alcohol is doing to them, and will have to understand the disease concept. Even though it may be easier to get well once the problem is acknowledged, the older person usually perceives drinking in terms of morality and sin so that secretiveness and shame become major hurdles to overcome.

AA can become, for the older person, a group functioning beyond the maintenance of sobriety. It can serve as an automatic
friendship network where people can meet and gain a sympathetic
ear for the asking. This can fill a special need for the bereft older
person who has suffered many losses and is now alone.

There will be more hope for recovery when additional social
supports are provided. Structured assistance is available from
many community agencies and includes visits from health aides,
transportation to and from meetings, shopping assistance, and
medical attention. Your concerns about elderly parents can be
ably dealt with by local councils on aging or bureaus of elderly affairs. By helping your parent help himself or herself, you will be
helping yourself too.

PART III

Climbing Out of the Trap

9
How Did It Happen?

We all come from the past, and children ought to
know what it was that went into their making, to
know that life is a braided cord of humanity
stretching up from time long gone, and that it
cannot be defined by the span of a single journey
from diaper to shroud.

Russell Baker, *Growing Up*

Trying to understand why alcoholism hit your family and not
another or why your sister is thriving and your brother is
drinking his way into oblivion is as hard as trying to unravel
a knotted ball of wool. But there are some studies and observations
that may help you find your way through the tangle.

Heredity Versus Environment

Every study of alcoholism down through the years shows a
much higher rate of alcoholism among family members than in the
general population. This used to be attributed to family disinte-
gration, or learned behavior, or poverty. Now a new emphasis has
been placed on the role of heredity, and some researchers expect
that a chemical basis will be found. But as Migs Woodside wrote
in her pioneering report *Children of Alcoholics*, prepared for the
governor of New York State: "The relationship of heredity and
environment is [. . . so] inextricably tangled. . . . While it is proba-
ble that certain genetic predispositions exist, it is also likely that
the quality of life in an alcoholic home may affect future alcohol-

ism. [At this time . . .] research in the field has been able to provide some signposts but no absolutes."

One of the signposts comes from studies of infants adopted soon after birth. Dr. Donald Goodwin of the University of Kansas Medical School found that sons of alcoholics were four times more likely to become alcoholic than sons of nonalcoholics, even if they had been separated from their alcoholic parents and reared by nonrelatives who did not drink excessively. Sons of nonalcoholic biological parents did not become alcoholics at a high rate even if they grew up in alcoholic foster families. The evidence for daughters was not so clear.

The importance of genetic factors is also supported by at least two studies (one in Finland, the other in the United States) which show higher concordance of alcoholism for identical twins (who share the same hereditary makeup) than for fraternal twins (who share no more than other brothers and sisters). But it is important to remember that not every identical twin with a brother who was alcoholic became alcoholic. So alcoholism is clearly not inevitable, even with a strong family tendency.

How is the tendency passed on? Several lines of research into the physical processes that might make one person more susceptible than another are being pursued. One biochemical study shows that, before they even start to drink alcohol, children of alcoholics, like established alcoholics, have depressed zinc levels in their blood. This suggests that some sort of metabolic process is askew even before heavy drinking begins. And familial studies indicate that hyperactive boys often have fathers who are heavy drinkers, pointing toward some neurochemical disorder. These hyperactive sons are more likely than their brothers to develop alcoholism later in life.

In another approach to the problem, scientists at Harvard Medical School found a little-known chemical—2,3 butanediol—in the blood of chronic alcoholics. It does not show up in the blood of nonalcoholics even after they have been drinking and is another link pointing to a metabolic disturbance in those who have become addicted to alcohol. Large portions of some populations (Orientals, for instance) have a sensitivity to alcohol that makes it unpleasant for them to drink. Even when they drink small amounts, many develop a facial flush and a general feeling of malaise. They are then automatically protected against alcoholism.

The Oriental reaction is one more indication that some built-in mechanism may involve enzyme differences in the liver.

The enzyme alcohol dehydrogenase helps produce acetaldehyde, the first step in the metabolism of alcohol. Dr. Mark Schuckit at the School of Medicine and Veterans Administration Center in San Diego has found preliminary evidence that levels of acetaldehyde are higher after drinking in both alcoholics and the nonalcoholic sons of alcoholic fathers than they are in the general drinking population. This suggests, says Dr. Schuckit, that acetaldehyde may combine with chemical neurotransmitters in the brain, causing them to produce a morphinelike substance that makes addiction likely.

More evidence that what happens in the brain plays a part in the development of alcoholism comes from research at the Downstate Medical Center in Brooklyn, New York, where studies of brain waves have shown that those at high risk for alcoholism have an abnormal brain wave known as P3. This implies that some electrical aberration in the brain may be inherited.

There is also the possibility that a supersensitive nervous system may be part of the inherited package that predisposes some people to alcoholism. Lynne Hennecke, a psychologist in private practice in New York City, found that the thirty children of alcoholics she tested had a heightened sensitivity to pain, sound, light, and environmental stimuli than did other children. A further study has shown that these "augmenters" learn to turn down the volume by using alcohol.

But clearly these chemical and nervous system clues are only a piece of the puzzle. They offer the hope of finding a possible avenue for prevention and treatment—a biological "marker" to determine who will and who won't get hooked. But the physical background of this disease is intertwined with other elements. Like diabetes and heart disease, alcoholism may have a genetic base, but certain environmental factors are needed to make the crucial difference between the appearance and nonappearance of active disease. And there are still those puzzling cases in which alcoholism appears, as it were, out of the blue with no family history to link it to hereditary factors.

Aware of the complexity of the problem, the National Council on Alcoholism has published a list of risk factors for the development of alcoholism. They are presented in no particular order, since even the experts do not agree on which are most important. You will probably find your own family has at least some of them:

- Families with a history of alcoholism, including parents, brothers, sisters, grandparents, uncles, and aunts.

- Families with a history of teetotalism. (Any extreme, either drinking too much or perceiving drinking as evil, may contribute to unhealthy drinking patterns.)

- Broken homes, particularly where there is parental discord or where the father is absent or rejecting.

- An ethnic background in which heavy drinking (often distilled spirits) is part of the cultural picture. For example, people of Scandinavian or Irish background are more likely to become alcoholic than those of Italian or Jewish descent. When neighbors and friends see drinking to excess as normal or at least acceptable, it is extremely difficult for a family to buck the tide, even when it knows well the dangers involved.

- Being the last child of a large family.

- Families with a high incidence of recurrent depression for more than one generation. (Alcoholism is found more frequently in males and depression more frequently in females in alcoholic families.)

- Families in which there is heavy smoking (although being a nonsmoker does not provide protection against alcoholism).

Corroborating the main elements of risk that others had identified, Dr. George Vaillant, author of *The Natural History of Alcoholism*, found "two significant precursors of alcoholism: (1) growing up in an alcoholic environment or one with ethnic drinking patterns conducive to abuse; and (2) having a number of close relatives with the illness."

Even with a high number of these risk factors in their backgrounds, most children of alcoholics do not become alcoholic themselves. Some stay away from alcohol entirely. Some have a brief period of heavy drinking, often in adolescence, and then go on to normal social drinking. Some repeat the family pattern and marry alcoholics. You may have tried to figure out what accounts for this high degree of variability, even within the same family. Researchers, too, have become intrigued and are trying to identify what factors make the difference.

Rituals as Predictors

One thing to consider is how your family handled and still handles holidays, vacations, and routine family meals. Dr. Steven Wolin at the George Washington University Medical Center for Family Research studied twenty-five families with at least one alcoholic parent and two grown children to assess whether the quality of these get-togethers predicted whether alcoholism would be passed on to the next generation. In some families the drinking did not disrupt family occasions. Either the alcoholic had not been included before the drinking became a problem, and therefore wasn't a part of the rituals anyway, or drunken behavior at these times was rare and generally ignored. In families in which the rituals remained intact, alcoholism was less likely to be passed on no matter how severe the drinking. In the families in which the rituals were disrupted, alcohol "changed the fabric of family life." These families tended to have the most alcoholism in the next generation.

Next, Dr. Wolin looked at adult children of alcoholics. Here he found, as any romantic knows, that marriage to the right person made the difference. The "right" person was one who did not come from an alcoholic home and whose ties to this nonalcoholic family were adopted by the adult child. One man said that one of the reasons he was attracted to his wife was because of her family's wonderful picnics! They were not just simple affairs where people throw hard-boiled eggs, tomatoes, and rolls in a paper bag and buy some Coke and beer on the way to the woods. On the contrary, half the fun was in getting ready, and each family member was responsible for part of the preparations. The picnic was planned for days as the site was chosen and the wicker baskets were packed. The food included the inevitable hotdogs but also featured such specialties as Italian pasta, shish kebab, and marinated chicken, beautifully arranged. These picnics were rituals; and this man knew how much he wanted them for his own children instead of the haphazard "outings with grub," which was how he characterized his own family's so-called picnics.

Even in families with disrupted rituals, only some of the children later become alcoholic or are seriously affected in other ways. Here's what is known about the factors or variables that make the difference. Some of them will be more significant for you than others, for they may have played a major role in your childhood.

Sex of Child and Parent

The son of an alcoholic mother is affected differently from a daughter and, by the same token, the daughter of an alcoholic father is affected differently from a son. (Recent evidence suggests that the daughters of alcoholic mothers suffer the most deleterious effects.) But it does not follow automatically that the daughter of a female alcoholic will follow in her mother's footsteps or that the son of a male alcoholic is more likely to become alcoholic than is his sister.

In one study of 1,930 alcoholics (410 of them women), 7 percent reported that they had an alcoholic mother and over 19 percent reported that they had an alcoholic father. In the same group of people, 18 percent of the men and 23 percent of the women had alcoholic fathers. Paternal alcoholism, it seems, is more likely to lead to alcoholism in children, both male and female. But women alcoholics are more likely to have a family history of alcoholism, and they are more than twice as likely as men alcoholics to have been brought up by two alcoholic parents.

Birth Order

It is not surprising to find that the youngest children in alcoholic families, particularly large families, are the ones who have suffered the most. The younger a child is when the alcoholism begins to affect family life, the more detrimental it will be to the child's health and development (assuming the alcoholic remains with the family). As you assess the variables that may have determined the degree to which you were affected by your parents' drinking, you may want to consider how old you and your siblings were when the drinking began and whether or not you were left alone to cope with its consequences.

Take the story of Brian. When he was away at college he began to receive phone calls from his younger brother and sister, who were at home with their mother. They would call him in the late evening and complain that she had passed out on the floor or that she had been hitting them with a broom. Brian had trouble believing their stories. He thought of his mother as the "perfect parent." She had functioned both as father and mother after her husband's death. (Brian was ten at the time.) She had always been there for him and the others when they needed her.

Now her drinking had escalated rapidly, and so did its harmful effects on the younger children. Brian's sister developed phobias and wouldn't go to school unless escorted by her mother; his brother started beating up other children in the building. After work Brian's mother would simply forget to fix anything for supper and would drink her own dinner. The children would eat what was available, straight from the refrigerator. If they bothered her, she would become enraged. It was during such a fit of anger that she had taken the broom to the children. Her violent behavior, totally uncharacteristic and unexpected, frightened the children and led them to call Brian.

The only child has a tough time too, because there are no built-in protections—no sisters or brothers around to soften the blows or explain what is happening—and options are limited when it comes to finding perceptive understanding. The child is stuck there all alone.

It is easier for older children to search for comfort. They are more able to ask for reassurance, and they may know where to go for it. They also have more freedom to move around and get out of the house. It follows then that, if the onset of the alcoholism is late, the child has a better chance to grow up with relatively "normal" parenting, at least during the nondrinking years.

Sally survived her adolescence by becoming active in a church group. She went to meetings three times a week, and by the time she was fifteen she decided that she wanted to go overseas as a missionary. She figured this would open an escape hatch for her. Her alcoholic father tried to wither her with his usual scorn: "They boil missionaries in oil, you know." But she stuck to her guns and continued her outside interest.

Those who leave to marry, to go to school, or to work, manage to bypass some of the detrimental effects of the drinking. But the younger ones, who still must depend on an alcoholic parent for daily needs, have a rough time.

Who Else Was There for You?

No matter how old you were when the drinking got bad, if you had someone there to help and support you, you probably were not as adversely affected as you would have been had you faced whatever was happening alone. Many adult children of alcoholics report that, when pressed, they were able to turn to others inside or outside the family to get what they needed. Research shows that those children who had a good relationship with at least one adult—a relative, parent of a friend, teacher, neighbor, older sister or brother, or hired housekeeper—tend to function best.

"I would have gone out of my mind if my grandmother hadn't been living with us," one man says. "She was like a buffer between all of us—not just my parents, but me and my parents and my sister and me too." Another man escaped serious damage because he found that he could turn to his mother, his nondrinking parent, for the love and guidance he needed. Sometimes the nondrinking parent gets a divorce, escapes the alcoholic chaos, and saves the children from further damage.

One man still talks about his father's friend who took him to all school functions. He particularly remembers that this man saw to it that he was always available when the annual Boy Scouts father–son dinner came along.

Good feelings about yourself can come from any number of people who are willing to listen and understand. And there can be variations on this theme, with children finding sustenance in surprising places. One young woman said that she would have felt alone in the world if it hadn't been for her three cats and a dog, who accompanied her to bed each night.

What Kind of Drinker Did You Live With?

Another factor that makes a difference in how you are affected by your parent's drinking is how your alcoholic parent behaved when he or she had had too much. If your father went to sleep whenever he was drunk, you were affected differently than if he had beaten up the family, kicked the dog, and been generally destructive or violent. If your mother managed to stay sober most of the day but collapsed at dinner time, you were affected differently than if she had begun her drinking at the breakfast table.

The family that suffers the most, of course, is the one in which there is violence. Amy says that before her parents got a divorce her home became a "war zone." She shared a room with her mother, and when her father returned from the bar he would try to beat down the door. The two of them would duck past him and run down to the basement, but he would follow. Once, she said, he threatened her mother at gunpoint while he used Amy as a hostage. After that incident she escaped from the danger at home by running away. She found work in a department store in a neighboring town, but soon racked up such a spotty work record that she lost her job. Fear of her father's overt rage kept her from contacting her parents and she finally ended up in the hospital with a diagnosis of "depression." After two months she was discharged from the psychiatric service there and, with the help of outpatient treatment, Al-Anon, and supportive friends, she began to get well.

Many people who drink do not become so clearly menacing. Nonetheless, some studies have shown that between 60 percent and 80 percent of criminal acts occur when either the perpetrator or the victim has had too much to drink. Faulty judgment and the loosening of inhibitions against unsanctioned behavior are common consequences of the action of alcohol on the brain.

It is natural that alcoholics who become docile when they drink are less threatening as parents. In fact, some children of alcoholics actually want their parents to stay drunk because in that condition they are more malleable and less frightening. One teenager said her father would set curfews for her when he was sober but would be oblivious to time and regulations when drunk. Some children go so far as to encourage their alcoholic parent to stay drunk by fixing drinks or going to the refrigerator for an asked-for beer. One man says he brought drinks to his bedridden father just to keep him quiet.

Social and Economic Status

It is painful for any family to lose self-respect and status. But the family that has financial resources and social stability is likely to weather the buffeting of an active alcoholic more successfully than one that has only meager resources. Economic stability makes a difference because more help is usually available to those who can afford it. The indigent have less chance to recover.

In some instances, however, the presence of wealth serves only to enable a family to cover up or, at most, to lessen the consequences of the drinking. One woman said that the fact that her mother was constantly drunk at home didn't really matter. There were servants who ran things very smoothly, preparing meals and caring for the four children and a multitude of pets. They even kept appointments straight for the entire family and saw to it that the children got to school and to their medical appointments and lessons on time. Not until her mother drove off the road with one of the youngsters in the back of their station wagon did her father take the car keys away. It was soon after this incident that her mother realized the seriousness of her drinking problem and went for help.

Family Attitudes

No matter what their economic status, some families view drinking as part of everyday life. For other families, drinking is an incidental part of life, to be taken or left alone; and in about one in five families, there is no drinking whatsoever. Clearly, how alcohol is used or not used within the context of the family must affect every young person.

In a family where everyone drinks regularly, where drinking too much is acceptable, and where no stigma is attached to overt drunkenness, the child develops attitudes that are specifically related to his or her perception of what drinking means in this particular family. Joseph came from a family in which daily drinking played a pivotal role. Each afternoon, after work, his parents were joined at the local bar by friends, most of whom came from the surrounding neighborhood. There they would remain into the night, drinking, talking, laughing, and eventually going home drunk, to flop into bed. Joseph spent afternoons after school in the bar too. Since he was not permitted to drink, he passed the time putting nickels into the jukebox and daydreaming. His brother, who was six years younger, had much more trouble amusing himself in the café. He would nag and make a pest out of himself and was always finally sent home. It was Joseph's task to run home occasionally—a block away—to check on him and help him get something to eat. Together they would open a can of corned beef or soup and would eat their dinner, each dipping a spoon into the can.

Joseph, like most children, never questioned his parents' way of life. It was accepted by the entire family and it went on, uncurtailed and uncriticized. However, at the age of thirteen, he discovered a way to enrich his daydreams: He found the library and began to read voraciously. With encouragement from a teacher, he escaped from his dreary home life into books. Today Joseph is a teacher, but his younger brother, who bore the brunt of the neglect, is a jobless alcoholic. His parents, who miraculously remained together in spite of mounting stress on their life together, died of cirrhosis of the liver in their early fifties. In a home such as this, the child is sure to be permanently affected.

The role of drinking is entirely different in another family—the Webbs. Here people drink on special occasions and sometimes at meals. Drinking never becomes a reason for gathering together, nor does it determine the making or breaking of a party. The statement "I need a drink" is unlikely to come from a member of this family. One is much more likely hear, "Let's have wine to celebrate"—an anniversary, a good potato crop, the birth of a grandchild. In the Webb family, drinking carries no sense of urgency or necessity. A take-it-or-leave-it attitude prevails and drunkenness is never condoned or overlooked.

In contrast to the Webbs are those families that never drink at all. They probably condemn, on moral grounds, all who do. They may look down on their drinking neighbors and feel a kind of moral superiority to them. This moralistic attitude toward drinking may be as hard on the children as Joseph's parents' everyday drinking was on him. The child sees others enjoying drinking, reads ads promoting drinking, and gets the message that alcohol can lead to happiness and will satisfy any dream. Children from abstaining families are likely, sooner or later, to explore the drinking life themselves. Then they easily get into trouble, because they haven't built up knowledge about alcohol or learned how their own bodies react to the drug.

In the Jones family, Tom's father was a minister. The "evils of booze" was a frequent subject of his sermons. He prayed for those who had fallen victim to alcohol—and for their families. Because Father Jones wanted to make sure that his son would not be plagued by the same torments that he witnessed daily in so many of his parishioners, he promised him $500 for his twenty-first birthday if he would abstain until that date. It took a great deal of strength on Tom's part not to drink at all, particularly because all his friends had been partying for years. Over that time, Tom had been the butt of a lot of ribbing. However, he successfully managed not to succumb to constant barrages of pressure from his peers, and on his twenty-first birthday he was rewarded with $500 along with warm congratulations from his father.

After his birthday party, he joined his friends in the local bar and drank himself into a stupor. After that he got drunk every time he drank at all. He had never learned his own limits and couldn't understand why alcohol affected him so powerfully. Soon his drinking was out of control. Three years to the day after his first drink, he was escorted by his stunned father to an alcoholism treatment center.

In assessing what happened in your home and how you might have been affected, ask yourself these questions:

Was drunkenness condoned?

How strong was the pressure for adults to drink?

Were there sanctions against drinking? By whom and why?

How and when were you introduced to alcoholic beverages?

How strong were negative attitudes toward drinkers?

What was said or done about drunk people?

Was every day a drinking day?

Ethnic Attitudes

Your responses to the questions above may be affected by the attitudes prevalent in the ethnic group into which you were born. For example, in groups where drunkenness is condoned or at least not abhorred, alcoholic beverages are used freely and people become addicted unwittingly. Lack of awareness of the trouble they may bring upon themselves and their families contributes to the high rate of alcoholism in these groups. This is true in many Irish-American communities and in communities of people with Scandinavian backgrounds.

Alcoholism among Jews is a different story, for drunkenness is generally unacceptable and unexpected in Jewish families. Yet when Dr. Sheila Blume, former director of the New York State Division of Alcoholism, was doing research on Jewish alcoholics, she found, much to her surprise, that many of them had a relative, often in another generation, who had had a drinking problem. These were new findings because alcoholism had been thought to be rare among Jewish people. Dr. Edgar Levenson, a psychoanalyst, speculates half-jokingly on what might have been the "protective mechanism" for many people of this background. He writes in *The Fallacy of Understanding,* "this family constellation—that is, an aggressive, domineering, seductive mother and a weak, passive, undermining father—is characteristic for the alcoholic. But this is also the classic Jewish family structure. So, it is asked, why are there so few Jewish alcoholics? The answer is, of course, their mothers won't let them."

Obviously, this mechanism doesn't always work. And now that the question is really being investigated, the number of Jewish alcoholics, though still comparatively small, seems larger than had been assumed. So the real issue may not be whether their mothers let them drink but whether they let them talk about it—especially outside the family.

Community Attitudes

Some drinking parents are not condemned by their community. In fact, they are joined and supported by it. Had these parents lived in a dry town or in a Mediterranean country, their lifestyle might have been frowned upon. But social life in most of America takes place as people gather in drinking spots. The cocktail hour, the drink with a business luncheon, the beer while watching sports events, and the wine with dinner are all acceptable drinking customs here. In the suburbs people are most likely to drink heavily at parties at home or in clubs. In cities there are bars on streetcorners and pockets of people who will sanction drunkenness. In rural areas, nearly every community has its spot where people meet and drink.

No matter where the drinking takes place or what its style, the child is inevitably a witness to it, if not a party to it. That child must be affected to one degree or another by what he or she lives with and sees daily. But there is a way that some children are affected by parental drinking even before birth!

The Fetal Alcohol Syndrome

Children of mothers who drink heavily (and perhaps even moderately) during pregnancy may be affected by the alcohol that gets to them through the placenta. Alcohol ingestion during pregnancy can cause low birth weight, retardation, and other birth defects. There is conflicting evidence about the dangers of moderate drinking during pregnancy (although the federal government advises pregnant women not to drink at all), and there is some indication that even a few drinks may help precipitate miscarriages. Allan Luks, executive director of the Alcoholism Council of Greater New York, estimates that 10 percent of all alcohol-caused birth defects are associated with as little as two drinks a day. The full range of defects—mental retardation, distinctive facial features, heart problems—is called fetal alcohol syndrome (FAS) and is linked to women who have five or more drinks a day. Some children without the full syndrome show reduced intellectual capacity. This is more true of boys than of girls and may be another indication that the male of the species is more vulnerable than the female. And it may not be the mother alone whose alcohol consumption affects the fetus. Some physicians postulate that heavy drinking may damage sperm and produce miscarriages.

Born Drunk

There are reports of babies who have literally been "born drunk." Their mothers were drinking when labor began and may have continued in order to kill the pain. Since the bloodstreams of mother and child are so close until the umbilical cord is severed, the baby has the same blood alcohol level as the mother until birth. These babies need to be "detoxified" as they come into the world, and they apparently go through some of the same physio-logical traumas that adults experience when the blood alcohol level drops suddenly. This is hardly a healthy way to begin life, whether or not it is simply the result of the mother's one drinking episode or part of an alcohol bath that the baby has lived in for nine months. Pregnant mothers need to know that when they drink, the fetus drinks too. There is speculation that this exposure to alcohol in the uterus predisposes the child to later addiction and could be just one more path leading to the intergenerational trap.

10

Coping and Changing

You know what heals? Seeing someone who's had
an even worse time than you've had and who's
made it and is living the kind of life you'd like to
live.

Don, Age 30

N ow that you know the part alcoholism played in your family
in making you what you are, how can you go about making
the changes that will help you cope well and feel better?
The first step is to identify and understand what happened to you
as you were growing up. The next is to consider what you, as an
adult, can do about the shadows these early experiences still cast
on your present life.

And there is good news. Research (and common sense) show
that children who are reared under dire circumstances can grow
up to be competent adults in spite of the turmoil they experienced
during childhood. Preliminary results from the twenty-year longitudinal study of children of alcoholics by Dorothy Miller and Michael Jang in San Francisco pinpoint some escape routes. "For
example," they write, "if a subject has a successful marriage and
manages to attain a good education, get a good job, or find a different lifestyle, he will escape the intergenerational trap. Yet all of
these achievements are subject to luck and chance and cannot be
predicted by the data available to the social scientist."

No one could have predicted what happened to Marty. Now in
his thirties, he began as a Family Hero but couldn't keep up with

the demands he made on himself. Eventually he became a drug addict in New York. But, being the child of an alcoholic proved to have its advantages. Today, as a remarkably effective counselor to others, he says, "It made me a more compassionate and understanding person. I'm now grateful for what I had to go through because suffering is the admission ticket to human growth. I look at my friends who have not suffered and their lives seem sterile."

There are other families in which one parent turns out to be so strong he or she can supply the children with enough love and effective guidance to keep them relatively unscathed. Greg's mother drank heavily during most of his childhood. However, his father managed his own life so that he could give his son an enormous amount of care and attention. He picked him up after school, encouraged his studies, took him on summer camping trips, and saw to it that he had the clothing he needed during the year. Most important, he loved him and told him so. Greg, now twenty-seven, appears by all standards to be an effective, happy person who is coping well.

Shaking Family Roles

Even if you didn't have this kind of life-net in growing up, you may be doing well. But some childhood coping patterns may have become inappropriate and are now candidates for change. Before you can make permanent changes, you have to identify these old patterns.

For example, until you were in your late teens you may have felt good being the Family Hero, but now you don't get as much satisfaction from that role. So what was once rewarding has to be unlearned because it is no longer applicable or helpful. And it's hard to unlearn something that at one time got you the gravy. You hang on to it not only because it is a habit but because you are still convinced that it will work. Calling attention to yourself by lighting matches was dangerous but successful when you were a child, but now, even though it may not be so dangerous, it is far from successful. There have to be more mature ways of making your presence known.

One young therapist working with young children of alcoholic parents recalls that he combined the Mascot with the Family Hero role when he was growing up. He fooled around a lot to get attention, but he worked hard and got good grades too. Now, he says, he is still playing these two roles, but using them productively. In working with victims of family disruption he uses puppets, role playing, and other theatrical devices that give free reign to his long experience as the family "ham."

Another man has contracted with his family to give him time alone each day just to sit in his study and think. His interludes are a much-needed respite from household commotion. When he was a child he would crouch, curled up, under the staircase in order to have time away from the hubbub. It would certainly be peculiar, even eccentric, for a fifty-seven-year-old to huddle under the stairs. The daily time-out in his study serves the same safety-valve purpose.

Another man recognized himself as the Quiet One, always giving in to others and taking a back seat in life. When his boss at the computer company put his name out of alphabetical order at the bottom of a program that his group had designed, he was able to muster up the courage to insist that he be appropriately recognized. This new-found ability to assert himself made him feel more valuable immediately, without going through a lengthy process of assertiveness training. It also had positive repercussions in other areas of his life. He went home and told his children, in no uncertain terms, to get their clothing out of the living room and to remove their toys from the front doorway. Such commands would previously have been deferred to his wife.

Charles Deutsch, a psychologist and author of *Broken Bottles, Broken Dreams,* offers other ways in which childhood coping roles can be altered or abandoned. He suggests that the Family Hero change by learning to let go, to relax and stop doing it all. He maintains that the Scapegoat will not be able to come to terms with his own problems until he sees that his parents' drinking was abnormal. Then he must realize that its consequences are still the source of his anger and that he is still acting this out daily in anti-social, self-destructive ways. Deutsch suggests that the Lost Child needs help to express wants and anger and needs to be given hope, for it is essentially the feeling of hopelessness that holds him back. Last, he suggests that the Mascot learn to take himself more seriously and then go on to find productive ways to use pent-up energy without resorting to chemicals.

Coping Versus Escaping

The difference between coping and escaping is not clear to children of alcoholics who have learned to function, either by example or by inference, by doping themselves up, denying, or ignoring. In the long run, escaping doesn't work. It buries feelings that later may reveal themselves in physical illness; it diverts attention from tasks at hand that later get pushed aside and often multiply when they are ignored. And for the highly vulnerable adult children of alcoholics, self-medication for anxiety can easily lead to dangerous use of drugs and alcohol.

When you think about yourself, are you running away from your troubles or are you coping constructively? These questions may help:

1. If something upsets you, do you pretend that you didn't hear it or that you really don't care?

2. If you are angry, do you keep quiet until you feel as if you are going to explode?

3. If you feel uneasy with strangers, do you withdraw into a corner or avoid situations in which there are people you don't know?

4. Do you protect yourself by putting others down, lowering their self-esteem and doing nothing positive for yourself?

5. Do you act out your fury from the past on those you love today?

If you answered yes to even one of these questions, you are reacting rather than coping well. There are more constructive ways to deal with your feelings.

If You Are Still Angry

There's no doubt about it, having a parent who drinks too much is infuriating. And that anger does not go away automatically as you grow up. However, there are ways that people successfully work off steam. Here are some you might want to try—after, of course, counting to ten first:

1. Yell out the window (if there are no nearby neighbors).

2. Hit a pillow or a punching bag.

3. Go for a brisk walk (or run).

4. Close the car windows and scream.

5. Take a shower or a bath. Go for a swim.

If none of these is helpful, begin now to look for ways to let go that will do the trick specifically for you. It may be something you've never thought of before, but if it works, stick with it! Do not: take a drink, speed down the street, take a pill, or pull out your hair.

If you still find that you're reenacting the argumentative style of your parents, you may need to look more thoroughly for the origins of that style in order to drop it. The daughter of two alcoholics attributes her battling tendencies to the fact that she heard nothing at home but her parents' incessant arguing, and saw nothing more than their bizarre behavior. "One day my father set fire to the toilet paper and threw the fireball down the stairs. Another time my mother tossed our little dog across the room and then slapped my brother for leaving his bike outside unattended. And then they blamed each other for the ruckus."

This kind of irrational behavior illustrates an operating mode that you should be conscious of so that you won't repeat it mindlessly. One way to do that is to check your present life for friction:

1. Tape your family at the table.

2. Tape a conversation as you and whomever you live with prepare to go out.

3. Notice ways other families have of asking each other for favors, discussing what TV channel to look at, or deciding what to have for dinner.

4. Identify any persistent argumentative pattern. Fights often arise over the same thing year after year. For example, one married couple of thirty years say they still snap at each other when it comes to who's going to drive.

The important thing is to identify the areas of conflict and negotiate or talk about how you feel, without putting the emphasis on what's being done *to* you. For adult children of alcoholics, talking about feelings, even feeling feelings, is new and difficult, so they often have to start from scratch. It certainly is understandable if you are still angry at your parent who drank too much. At the same time, you may still be deeply hurt by your nonalcoholic parent—a father who paid the bills and "enabled" your mother to drink or a mother who slaved to keep the family together. Anger at the nonalcoholic is much more difficult to deal with because it doesn't appear warranted. And it is also difficult to acknowledge anger toward the person on whom you had to depend. Burying or denying these feelings could have made you even angrier.

A woman who has had years of therapy has just recently been able to face her anger at her nonalcoholic father. "He could run the world, or at least that's what I felt when I was a child. So why couldn't he run his own life and protect us? Although he was there, I felt abandoned. I'm still angry, but I feel guilty about the anger."

If You Are Still Feeling Guilty

Some of the guilt that results from having lived with a parent who drank too much can be dispelled. How does that happen? First of all, you need to be convinced that there is (or was) absolutely no connection between your parent's drinking and what you did or did not do. You can think of it in simple terms: If your father had cancer, would your having taken too much time in the bathroom have made any difference? If your mother had broken a wrist, would neglecting your teeth have changed the situation? You need to do away with the outrageous non sequiturs you grew up with and face reality; try to figure out what really caused certain things to happen. Illness is not necessarily caused by the behavior of family members. However, ingrained guilt that has been programmed into your thought processes for years is hard to wipe out, no matter what the realities are.

One man says that he was brainwashed by his alcoholic father, who said, "You take up too much room on this earth!" Ever since, he has felt guilty about his very existence. One woman lives with such overwhelming guilt that she can't look anyone in the eye; she says that she always feels like a fraud and apologizes for what she does before she does it.

Once you are convinced that you did not cause the drinking, then what? If your parents are still alive you may be able to talk to them to check on your own view of what actually did happen. You can also talk to relatives to see how they perceive what went on. Do they too really believe that you caused the alcoholism? They may be able to reassure you that the fighting you heard was not about you.

To deal with ingrained guilt feelings you may need to consult a therapist or clergyman, particularly if those feelings remain after you know intellectually that you are not guilty and that your guilt is inappropriate.

There is one special category of guilt that is written about in relationship to the Holocaust and to Hiroshima but that often goes unrecognized by people from alcoholic families: survivor's guilt. Children of alcoholics sometimes see themselves as survivors and wonder, "Why me?" That feeling comes from the false assumptions that you succeed only at the expense of someone else and that if you had only been better all this wouldn't have happened. This magical thinking presupposes universal fairness and order and demands that some sort of inevitable cosmic arithmetic exist.

A man from a huge family riddled with alcoholism says, "Now I realize why I give all my extra money away and still work three jobs. I just don't feel I deserve anything for myself when the others in my family are all failing in one way or another." This is a tough problem to work out because the origin of the distress is somewhat obscure. Even when you recognize the realities, the feelings may stay with you. In group therapy (see Chapter 11, "Getting Help") the burden is lightened by the knowledge that other people admit to the same or similar wishes and fantasies. Expressing in the presence of others what is usually unspeakable, can go far to reduce distressing or sensitive emotions.

If you are still upset by what seems to be an overload of guilty feelings and you don't have access to a group or a professional guide, it may be time to talk to a close friend. The guilt may have gone underground, only to appear unexpectedly in relationship to mundane matters: "Am I doing the right thing? Did I say the wrong thing? How should I have acted? Was I polite enough or did I hurt someone's feelings? Was I wearing the right clothing?" Friends can put these situations in perspective. Of course, in consulting friends, you take the risk of being embarrassed or chastised. If, for example, someone were to say, "Well, I wouldn't be seen wearing running shoes to a classy restaurant," or "Were you stuck to your seat in church when everyone else was rising?" you may be upset. But remember, these are inconsequential matters that may be momentarily embarrassing but that certainly should not give rise to any guilt; they happen to everyone. With friends you may be able to sort out what matters and what does not; with a therapist you will be able to do the same, but perhaps go into more depth to make changes that will help you feel more accepting of yourself.

Those who experience God as forgiving have a powerful way to rid themselves of guilt; both confession and prayer serve that purpose. A minister, priest, rabbi, or pastoral counselor can be enormously helpful when you feel overwhelmed.

If You Are Still Trying to Take Charge of Your Own Life

There's an old joke about a woman who claims decision making is no problem in her family. She says, "My husband makes the big decisions and I make the little ones. Like I decide what we name our children, where we live, what kind of car we buy, and who our friends are. But my husband decides who we vote for, what we do about the nuclear freeze, and what our stance is on international matters."

More seriously, most children of alcoholics are not so sure of themselves. Making decisions and changes become major issues, and many look for techniques to make it easier. One helpful way is to set aside time each day to keep a record or diary of your choosing experiences and methods—those times when you must make choices and how you arrive at decisions. Doing this will make you conscious of the process and you'll find that some decisions are automatic, like drinking orange juice at breakfast or putting the cat out before you go to work. But others take more conscious consideration, particularly those that have to do with jobs, marriage, geographic changes, and relationships with children and parents.

A way to strengthen and clarify your decision making is to experiment, step by step, with small shifts so that when you come to the larger ones they won't seem so momentous. (As someone once said, you can eat an elephant if you take one bite at a time.) Another, more concrete way to make changes is to follow this six-step process:

1. Define the problem.

2. Set a goal for making a change.

3. Gather information or data that habitually prevents you from attaining your goal or making changes.

4. Create an action plan, a way to attain your goal.

5. Check yourself to see if you are making changes or progress toward attaining the goals you have set.

6. Anticipate difficulties so that the supports you need will be close at hand. Be honest with yourself.

Because so many children of alcoholics have trouble with substance abuse, including food, here's an example of how an older woman used this system to lose weight and control food binges that had been going on for a lifetime. First she defined the problem: "I'm twenty pounds overweight and my ankles hurt when I walk and my skirts are getting tighter." Then she set a goal for herself, which was to lose twenty pounds by cutting calories to fewer than 1,200 a day. Next she defined the possible pitfalls and cautioned herself not to eat in restaurants, not to have sweets in the house, and not to become overtired, which she knew inevitably led to eating sprees. Then she wrote down an action plan, which included counting calories, writing down everything she ate, talking to friends who also had eating problems, and attending weekly Overeaters Anonymous meetings. She then checked herself by weighing in weekly and by testing her walking endurance. Last, she reinforced her commitment to honesty by checking calories each day and finding a special friend to talk to about feelings and temptations. Thus she brought the difficulties into focus so as not to deny or ignore the problem.

If this particular system is not one that appeals to you, there are other ways to help yourself. One possibility is to begin by picking out one of two items that you designate more important:

- Do you want to keep your car in good order and running, or would you rather win friends by lending it?

- Would you rather read a good book or catch up on today's news?

- Would you rather cook a meal for ten or send out for pizza?

- Given a limited amount of time, would you rather write to your congressman to promote disarmament or straighten out your checkbook?

Now take a slightly more complicated process. Pick five items and list them in order of personal preference:

- An evening at the bowling alley.

- A trip to the zoo.

- A long walk.

- A good movie.

- An evening alone watching TV.

The items above are so broad that they may not cause you much difficulty. But what do you do when there are more complications or more at stake? For example, what should you do about Mother's Day?

- Call your mother.

- Go see your mother.

- Send your mother a card.

- Send your mother flowers.

- Skip the whole thing.

You may want to make up your own lists to reflect your personal concerns and interests.

Itemized lists such as these do nothing more than clarify. You won't see the answers come up on a computer screen and you can't rely on equations to make decisions that could lead to life-long changes. Keep in mind, however, where your own well-being comes on your list of priorities. Some children of alcoholics leave themselves off all lists, and many keep themselves from making decisions because they fear failure or feel they are not entitled to have what they want or need. They feel they are not worthy in some way or will make the wrong choices no matter what.

What if you think, "These ideas sound great, but if I knew what I wanted I'd go for it." Or "I don't even know where to begin." Some people find that talking to others helps them get started on their own thinking. Sometimes, too, another person provides a model to imitate, filling in the gaps that have come from living in chaos. As you succeed in making choices that are appropriate and right, you will gain self-confidence, which in turn can lead to a wonderful sense of self-mastery. As you become conscious of choosing and changing, your sense of being in control will be enhanced, and you will feel better and thus more able to trust others and yourself.

If You Still Can't Trust

Trusting others is risky business. If you became skeptical early in life, it's incredibly difficult to develop faith later on. However, with persistence, it can be done. In general, lack of trust breeds self-doubt, so it only makes sense to look more deeply into how serious those doubts are. They may mean nothing more than that you are extremely sensitive or unusually curious about yourself. If you feel out of joint or disconnected, it's always a good idea to find out more, for no other reason than to reassure yourself. An overpowering sense of insecurity may be indicative of pathology and should be reviewed with a psychiatrist, psychologist, or other mental health worker. Then, if there is a serious problem, you will be in touch with someone who can help.

If you had a toothache, you surely wouldn't hesitate to find the cause of the discomfort. You would do something about it right away before the pinpoint cavity became a deep hole or the tooth died. However, mental health concerns are more subtle and still so stigmatized that people are loath to go for help when the pain is only slight; they go only when they can't bear it any longer.

You can, of course, try to get out of the no-trust bind on your own. As you attempt it, begin, as usual, by taking small steps:

1. Purposefully share a confidence with an adult friend. Try to see what it feels like to trust someone else.

2. Let someone borrow something of value, but don't go out on a limb. (Keep the value of the article within reasonable limits.)

3. Invite someone to your home whom you would not ordinarily invite.

4. Let someone drive your car.

5. Let someone plan a trip for you. (Choose the person carefully. Adult children of alcoholics often set things up so that failure is built in.)

6. Let go—take off your watch.

The person you choose to trust may not be trustworthy. You will be taking a chance, but in the long run trusting is rewarding and can make for the closeness you may still be looking for.

You might also do some thinking about whom you mistrust the most and why. Is the reason related to the drinking that affected your early life? Try to remember incidents that led to mistrust and see if you can link them to the drinking. Think of a specific disappointment that you had: Was someone drinking too much when it happened?

Like trusting others, trusting yourself is a huge stumbling block for adult children of alcoholics. When it comes to sizing up anything or anyone, they are never sure because their experience has been filled with misjudgments that often go back to a parent who could not fulfill commitments. If disappointments continue through their adolescence and young adulthood, they will need to put in time and work to overcome the damage.

How do you begin? Try going to a movie or an art show with a friend. Share thoughts about it. Note if you both come out with the same perceptions. Did you see the same things? Have similar feelings? Can you trust yourself to share how you felt? Any time you can check yourself out against the people around you to counteract your self-doubts, you have a chance to find a more "normal" model than you had at home.

Another way to learn to trust yourself is by making small, inconsequential or reversible changes:

1. Move your bed from one side of the room to the other.

2. Wear a new color or combination.

3. Come home a different route.

4. Get a new pet.

5. Try a new tool or gadget.

6. Try saying no when you would ordinarily say yes.

If You Are Still Lonely

Remaining aloof, not trusting yourself and others, and therefore continuing to feel alone will only lead to more craving for friendship or intimacy. One way to start overcoming solitude is to hunt for others in an active, positive way. People will not fall from the sky into your lap, so at least half the effort will have to come from you. It may seem like the obvious thing, but try it anyhow: Sign up for a course, join a club or community activity, chat with a neighbor. Remember that one reason people join organizations and groups is because they feel alone and isolated, and they too are searching for others.

Right now you may feel that reaching out is impossible because it is so frightening. You don't know how to find friends or a group; you don't know whom to call, and you've never done anything like this before. What will you say if you do muster up the courage to call someone? Perhaps you will feel easier about it if you pretend, for your first try anyhow, that you are calling for a friend or to get information for someone else. An impersonal approach may keep you from becoming tongue-tied. Generally, people you call who are involved with education, community or neighborhood groups, or therapy will be understanding and eager to help. They've had lots of experience with people who are timid about picking up the phone or asking for information. A church or synagogue is another good place to begin. Religious organizations always need help and welcome new members and interested volunteers. The sooner you begin, the sooner your days of being an involuntary loner will come to an end.

When you do feel alone, there are ways to get away from the loneliness temporarily, even though eventually you will have to face it. Escaping is not destructive, but it is not a solution either. Once in a while, delaying the resolution will solve the problem. Reading, studying, watching television, doing puzzles, going to the movies or the theater (or whatever interests you) are the kinds of solitary disentanglements that provide distraction for a while. Later you will need to deal more positively with the aloneness.

Our social structure generates isolation, so that often people have to work to connect with neighbors. And loneliness appears to be universal among children of alcoholics. As you try to connect with others, remember that the rest of the world is not necessarily going to treat you as your family did.

Feeling Better about Yourself

If your reputation with yourself is not so good, you probably have been brainwashed by your family, society, or both. When people get it into their heads that they can't do certain things, they tend to fulfill that prophecy. To break the link, begin optimistically with new tasks and give yourself some that have built-in success potential so that in small ways you will gain a knowledge of who you really are and what you can do. Then you will feel more certain about your capabilities.

It is important to set reasonable goals because some of your feelings of low self-worth or self-doubt may stem not only from having experienced so many failures but also from having had a parent who viewed you as worthless.

Therefore, give yourself credit for successes, no matter how small they are. Don't make light of it if you are, for example, able to change the tire on your car. Pat yourself on the back. That's an accomplishment, even though others can do it too. Don't undervalue the skill you have—whether it's typing, driving, teaching, listening, playing music, or directing traffic at a school crossing. And don't bother comparing what you do well or how well you do it with what other people can do. You will only be undermining yourself. Your positive feelings cannot be born of competition, but must come from an internal sense of mastery. You really can't go out and look for self-esteem; it is a by-product of being able to do and cope.

Perhaps you are unrealistic and still try to reach the impossible goals set for you by your family. Barbara, now forty-seven, remembers with horror her high school graduation. She was third in a class of over 250. Her mother refused to attend the graduation ceremonies, claiming that she was ashamed of her daughter, who "should have been first in the class." When parents are insatiable because of their own feelings of inadequacy, they can never be totally content with their children's accomplishments.

That critical message may have been paraded before you daily with no chance of being corrected. But you can correct it now:

1. If you have always felt science and math were impossible for you, try solving some *simple* mathematical puzzles. You won't find out suddenly that you're a mathematical genius, but you may discover that you can understand much more than you thought you could.

2. If you have always felt inept in the kitchen, try a *simple recipe.* Again, you may surprise yourself (and those with whom you live).

3. If you have always felt physically awkward, practice one *simple exercise* until you can do it easily.

4. If you've always had trouble managing time, write out a plan for the day, hour by hour; a plan for the week, day by day; a plan for the month, week by week. Seeing it in writing will help you stick to it.

5. If something in your home doesn't work, challenge yourself and see if you can fix it without calling in an expert such as a plumber, electrician, painter, or general handyman. Or try more technical fix-it jobs—a watch, a kitchen appliance, or a radio. Of course, keep in mind that you may end up with a pile of screws, nuts, and bolts.

6. Sew on a button; sew up a torn furniture cover; change the length of your pants or your skirt. Making small improvements can be disproportionately satisfying.

7. Don't give up. Try competing with yourself. Score higher at the bowling alley or at Scrabble; increase your jogging distance or decrease your time per mile. Play a more difficult piece of music. In other words, *stretch* yourself, not just physically, but mentally too.

8. If you want to feel more powerful, call the White House and tell Washington what you think, positively or negatively, about what's going on in the world. The White House Special Comments Number is (202) 456–2852. It's open Monday to Friday from 9:00 A.M. to 5:00 P.M.

Rediscovering the Past

Even though your parents may be relatively uninvolved in your daily life or may have died, you may still feel that you want to say something to them about what happened and how upset they made you (and probably still make you) feel. One way to do that is to write a letter to them and include in it all your resentments, fury, disappointments, smashed dreams, and anything else that still rankles. Positive feelings can go into the letter too.

In writing a letter that you know will never have to be delivered, you can say freely how you feel without fear of retribution or of hurting anyone. Writing is a way to let out pent-up anger. It also can justify anger by reducing self-doubts. People who have written such a letter say it had an immediate effect on them, giving them a sense of satisfaction and relief. Some say they finally felt validated and realized, as they wrote, that they were not necessarily the crazy one. Here's a sample letter a lawyer wrote to his father:

Dear Dad,

I know you loved me and I remember how special I felt holding your hand as we walked down the street in our neighborhood and the kids there watched you in your uniform. Then I thought I'd have a uniform when I grew up. I wanted to be just like you and maybe I'd walk down the same street and show off to the same kids who would then be grown up. I loved you then, dad, and I was proud of you.

But things changed. It is about that change that I'm writing now, and that seems long ago. I've wished a million times that I had talked to you when you could hear me. But then I know you couldn't have heard me because you couldn't listen. You were in a fuzz all the time. You died when the drinking began to take you away from me. In fact, I always talked about you in the past, even when you were still alive; once a kid asked me if you were gone for good. I guess I did my mourning for you when I was a teenager. You were there in body, but not for me as the father I wanted.

I'll stop being vague and write about what I remember. Once I asked you why you kept on drinking after you had had too much. You didn't answer. Mom said, "Don't you dare talk to your father that way." I didn't know why she was so edgy, but she kept the family myth and defended you all the way to your grave.

The admiration I had for you ended one evening, abruptly, at the table. I looked at you and there you sat drinking and drooling and not making sense at all. I saw that I had ended up with this sloppy guy who couldn't chew his food because his teeth were in wrong. I was left angry. And all of a sudden I didn't care. You had fallen from the pedestal and, for me, you were dead. When you, in fact, did die, I couldn't shed a tear. You had left me years earlier. Dad, you embarrassed me. I vowed I wouldn't grow up like you. I can't stand the thought of you slouched in the car seat next to mom; or snoring asleep on the living room couch when I came home from school; or careening into liquor stores to "pick up a little something"; or neglecting to zip up your fly; or getting up to pee at night; or shaking as you drank your morning coffee, often slipping gin into it; or burning another hole in the rug as you fell asleep smoking. I hated it all. I hated your smell. I'm furious that I couldn't have had a father who not only looked like a naval officer, but acted like one too. I couldn't trust you. I hated the man you became as you drank over the years. I hate alcohol for doing it to you.

And I'm angry at mom too. Why didn't she help you change? Why didn't she get up and leave? Why didn't anyone help us? We got help for every other health problem, beginning with my flat feet and including the cat's fleas.

I wish you could come back and answer those questions. I feel sad most of the time now. You were not the father I needed and wanted. I have my own life to lead now—and I'm trying.

John.

It is unfortunate that the art of letter writing has virtually disappeared with the invasion of the telephone. Fascinating personal history and family lore are all but lost these days. Much of the spirit and richness of our everyday lives will disappear with us. If you write a letter to a parent and keep it, perhaps it will be of interest to your descendants someday, and it may help them understand why the family is the way it is and why certain members drink the way they do.

If writing is difficult for you, there are other ways to get in touch with the past. A woman named Dawn located some friends of her parents who had moved away and with whom the family had lost contact. They painted a wonderful picture of her parents' early marriage and courtship—a view of them she had never known because of everyone's increasing preoccupation with her father's drinking. She had never before thought of her parents as young, in love, and with plans for their future. The realization that they had been real people, neither all bad nor all good, enabled her to forgive her father and to reduce both the overwhelming anger she had come to feel toward him and the sadness of having missed so much. Eventually she returned to look at the house in which she had lived until she was six years old. As she stood in front of it she was able to recapture forgotten memories of her happier life there.

One therapist with an unusual amount of inventive insight suggested that his patient, the son of an alcoholic woman who had died when the boy was sixteen, visit his mother's grave so he might have another chance to recapture her reality as a person and not just a stumbling drunk. He sat next to the grave recalling her name—Alice, not just mother—and he began remembering that this was a woman with a childhood of her own, a family of sisters and brothers and parents, a home, a marriage, a career as a piano teacher. He conjured up her face, her ways, her voice. Until the visit to the grave he had blanked out her reality. This experience tapped into his immense sadness and anger but enabled him to think of his mother as she had been over and beyond the drunkenness and sickness. After a second visit to the grave and additional weeks of therapy his anger began to let up. He started to feel a sense of relief as he remembered, not the drunk, but the fallible human being.

One woman brought back the past by returning to the town in which she was raised and spending a morning riding on the school bus. "I couldn't believe how vivid the memories were. I even felt that familiar tight feeling in my stomach. I could see my mother again, sitting on the step waving good-by. I knew now, but not then, that she was sitting down because she had little strength to stand. And she was waiting for us all to get out of the way so she could go back to her drunken sleep. And I remembered friends and how terrified I was that they wouldn't sit near me on the bus and how much I wanted them to think my dress was 'right.' But the bus ride brought back good things too—feelings of safety from the teacher and graham crackers and milk, the expected school snack. What a way to turn a blurry past into a solid memory!"

Another productive way to reach back into the past to further understand what really happened in your family is to search for an older relative—an aunt, an uncle, a cousin, a grandparent—who remembers the stories that have been passed down. Who were the family "characters"? What are the legends about your great-grandparents or grandparents? Are there photographs of your ancestors? In discovering your "roots," you may clear up some of the mysteries and uncover the trail of alcohol through the generations. A graphic way to do this is to draw a family tree, showing your parents' sides of the family and their ethnic origins. You may want to find out more about these groups and how they used alcohol. Was it part of their culture from the beginning? Did other people introduce alcohol to your ancestors? How is alcohol mentioned in stories, legends, or writings of that group? What were its daily practices and patterns? How do your parents' and your drinking patterns fit into the one that had its beginnings in history? If you are interested in further exploration of the past, data may also be available from historical societies, libraries, family records, and genealogy clubs or societies.

You can also try to revive forgotten memories through a technique known as guided imagery, or visualization. The proponents of this method reason that by using your present-day imagination to re-create the past, you get around the censorship of later years so that the surfacing images represent yourself and your emotions. Hypnotism may accomplish the same thing. However, keep in mind that these special techniques should be done with a well-trained guide or hypnotist.

A simpler way of remembering the past is to draw a picture of yourself as a child or adolescent. Then draw a picture of yourself with your family, describing what was going on as you draw. (Don't worry if you're not an artist.) No matter how you go about it, an odyssey into the past is an excellent way to bring back some of the pleasurable times and to correct distorted views.

Humility and Humor

Some people don't have to search so far back or so deeply. They are healed by time alone and no one knows why. The ease with which they recover may or may not have anything to do with their own efforts or another person's guidance. Some turn to religion as a way to cope with the harshness of the world. Prayer puts people in touch with the reality of God and provides a structure that makes things possible for people who feel empty. In the words of an adult child of an alcoholic: "Prayer is letting go to God, or whatever you want to call it. For us it is letting go of control; you don't have to control everything any more as most of us do. You come in touch with life power, a power that is greater than people. Prayer is listening, not asking. It is a spiritual, loving listening, and an acceptance of being loved and forgiven. We recognize that we are unique human beings; we are special, not different. We need to center on others rather than on ourselves, and then help comes from other people." However, prayer is not for everyone and there are some who cannot be comforted by belief in a higher power; it is simply not in their emotional vocabulary. They therefore have to look elsewhere for a source of contentment.

For some people, humor is the balm that makes coping possible. It releases tension, transforms big problems into little ones, and makes light of suffering. There certainly are times when it is a relief to laugh about the awfulness. Laughter disguises sad feelings and invites others to join in to alleviate the discomfort.

At times humor is the only way to ameliorate the unbearable reality of the Holocaust, the possibility of nuclear war, or the anguish suffered by the severely handicapped. (A bumper sticker reads: "One nuclear bomb can ruin your whole day.") Sometimes jokes make situations less weighty, less awkward, less embarrassing or humiliating. You have only to go to an AA meeting to hear jokes about alcoholic people that would not be acceptable or funny if they were told by outsiders. They represent a kind of battlefield camaraderie:

"I know all about alcoholism. I had it three times last summer."

"Alcoholism is caused by a Valium deficiency."

"I'd rather have a bottle in front of me than a frontal lobotomy."

"The difference between an alcoholic and a drunk is that the alcoholic goes to meetings."

Suicide

Suicide is not a way to cope, but in the minds of some it is the only solution. "I'm sort of apologetic about my existence. It was a mistake to start with. Why not end it?" is how the forty-year-old son of two alcoholics put it.

In the past twenty-five years there has been a meteoric rise in the suicide rate among young Americans, with an increase of over 250 percent among women and 300 percent among men. Two studies report evidence of alcoholism in about 30 percent of all suicides, but there are no figures on how many of those represent young people with alcoholic parents. Nor are there figures on the rate of suicide among adult children of alcoholics, but there are indications that any young person from an alcoholic home has a greater chance of becoming a suicide victim than his or her peer from a nonalcoholic home. Many adult children of alcoholics report that they have thought seriously about killing themselves, whether or not they drink too much. Some have slash scars on their wrists or talk about their attempts at overdosing. As the son of an alcoholic mother admits, "I've wondered, does everyone feel this way? How many people would rather be dead?"

According to David Reynolds and Norman Farberow, authors of *Suicide: Inside and Out,* "An essential precursor of suicidal behavior is a sense of powerlessness. There may be an overlay of anger or despair. . . . When people speak of the common associations between hopelessness and suicide or between despondency and suicide, they are referring, in part, to their shared feature, powerlessness." Considering how frequently hopelessness, despondency, powerlessness, and anger occur in adult children of alcoholics, it would be no surprise if the suicide rate among them were disproportionately high.

Everyone should be aware of the warning signs of suicide. People who are thinking about killing themselves may go from low to high moods quickly, without warning or explanation, as if all problems were suddenly solved. They may verbalize feelings: "I'm at the end of my rope." "What's to live for? I don't care." "No one loves me." "There's no way out." And the not so subtle "I wish I were dead." They may be discovered getting everything in order, preparing for the end. That is exactly what goes on in the 1983 Pulitzer Prize-winning play *'night, Mother* by Marsha Norman.

The young protagonist bluntly announces to her mother that she is about to kill herself and proceeds to make the preparations on stage as she tells her mother how she will do it, why, and when. It is the blatant "upfrontness" of this process that makes the play so powerful. Preparations for suicide are not ordinarily so openly discussed or demonstrated, unless a family is involved with a terminal illness and all members agree to condone the suicide.

If a friend or someone in your family mentions suicide, even laughingly, it is a serious matter and professional help should be procured as quickly as possible. First, do not leave the person alone. Then, for immediate help, call someone you trust—the police, the emergency room of the local hospital, an ambulance service, a local physician or clergyman or pastoral counselor. Or call a hot line listed in your phone book under suicide help lines or suicide prevention. If these do not exist in your community, a telephone operator may be able to connect you to an appropriate emergency resource. However, remember that it is always best to consider a way to get help *before* you need it!

Invulnerable Children

Perhaps you are not struggling with any of these problems or feelings. Or perhaps you have a brother or sister who seems to have escaped the bad effects of parental drinking. "Seems" is the important word here. It is difficult to find children from alcoholic homes who go completely unscathed. True, genetically some are stronger than others, brighter than others, or born with an uncanny ability to cope. And they may look very healthy, both physically and mentally. But the stressful coping ultimately takes its toll in problems relating to work, play, interpersonal relationships, and addictive behavior. The fact that "invulnerable children" become high achievers doesn't mean they are not plagued by the neurotic problems that stem from their early experiences in an alcoholic home. Their achievement may be just another inventive cover-up. If you look under the cover you will not necessarily find a stable adult.

This certainly does not mean that every child who lived with alcoholism will inevitably be unable to live a full, happy life. In fact, many recent studies support the view that children, in general, are less fragile and more resilient than people have thought.

When Dr. Stella Chess, the pioneering child psychiatrist, did a comprehensive review of studies that followed children from their early lives into adulthood she concluded that "we now have a much more optimistic vision of human development. The emotionally traumatized child is not doomed, the parent's early mistakes are not irrevocable, and our preventive and therapeutic intervention can make a difference *at all age periods*" (emphasis added). This is another way of saying that even if alcoholism happened in your family you have the power to break the generational link *now*, for negative experiences early in life can be remedied by better ones later on. And getting outside help can often make the difference.

11

Getting Help

Most people, when their car breaks down on the highway, either get out and fix it or call a mechanic. When my car had a flat tire, I called the suicide hot line.

Beth, Age 33

Not only do adult children of alcoholics have trouble asking for appropriate help; they often have difficulty asking for anything at all. Since they have been disappointed so many times and since they rarely received the assistance they needed as young children, it is not hard to understand why they are hesitant to ask for anything. In addition to wondering, "Why am I the way I am?" they ask themselves, "How did I get this way? Does everybody feel like this? How can I feel better?"

There are no easy answers to these questions. Becoming emotionally healthy does not happen instantly, like switching on the light to drive away the dark. It is a slow, difficult process—for, after all, the road you have traveled already has been a long one, full of bumps, curves, and hidden hazards.

You may need someone else's guidance along the way to understanding. In some areas, you may have to take what there is and the choices will be few; in others, the varieties of help may be bewildering. Whatever you try, give it a chance. Adult children of alcoholics are prone to switch from one thing to another, trying in a hurry to find the miraculous answers to the questions that plague them. One man says wryly, "We own more self-help books than any other group in the world."

Do You Need Therapy?

Because children of alcoholics have so much trouble trusting their own judgment and a lot of difficulty knowing what is normal, they may have doubts about their needs for therapy. Perhaps you think the way you feel is normal enough and you just want to do a patch job on yourself but skip any major excavation. One way to tell if you really need outside help is to listen to those close to you. If a friend, spouse, or loved one has hinted that you do, you should seriously consider it. Some people feel that seeking out help or therapy is a sign of weakness, shame, or guilt. Recognizing the need for help, however, is really a strength. It shows a self-awareness and a will to grow. If you decide it is indicated, it will be something you are doing for yourself and it will not in any way hurt or demean your parents or their memory.

Some of the clues to knowing you need help are feelings of depression, uncontrollable anger, and incapacitating fears or disorientation. Or you may repeatedly find yourself involved in interpersonal difficulties. If so, a professional counselor may be able to determine with you whether the stress under which you live can be diminished by therapy. Sometimes just one or two sessions are enough to help you make a decision. One young man described his dilemma: "My life was like a puzzle. I couldn't get all the pieces together. What's more, many pieces were blank and some weren't even there—they were missing! In therapy, as time went on, all the parts appeared and at some point they began to fit together." Another said, "I was ready to hang myself in the garage when a friend made an appointment for me with a therapist. 'If you love me,' she said, 'you'll keep this appointment.' So I went. And I'm still here."

Goals of Treatment

It has been said that the purpose of therapy is to make you more comfortable. What does that mean? Usually the goals include:

- Healing wounds from the past.

- Gaining a sense of worthwhileness and hope.

- Increasing your ability to protect and comfort yourself and those you love.

- Finding a way to rid yourself of unnecessary limitations.

- Developing a way to interact with the other people in your life.

- Enabling yourself to be more fully and clearly expressive.

- Finding a way to increase the extent of loving relationships.

- Ridding yourself of neurotic fears, compulsions, and self-destructive activities.

In other words, therapy is a way of getting to know why you behave the way you do and then finding new and fulfilling ways of being the kind of person you want to be.

David Treadway, associate clinical director of The Institute at Newton, Massachusetts, refers to the "lobster metaphor" when he talks about the process of therapy. He likens it to the stages a lobster goes through when it sheds a shell that doesn't fit any more. At the time the lobster is shedding, it is very vulnerable, easily hurt. As it grows a new shell that fits better, the lobster becomes less fragile and more able to protect itself.

The Resistances

What are the roadblocks that keep adult children of alcoholics from going out and hunting for what they need so badly? First, and perhaps the biggest one, is the risk involved in revealing the family secret. One therapist says it took over a year for a patient to report that her father was an alcoholic. When she finally acknowledged the alcoholism, the energy that had gone into hiding it was released so she then had much more to work with in therapy. She felt freer and more honest. It takes time to come to trust a therapist enough to talk about what a family has been hiding for so long.

Second, you may not feel you deserve any help. Many adult children have such a low sense of themselves that they believe the life they lead now is what they've bargained for, what God meant for them, what they should be happy with—things could be worse. One woman has been virtually brainwashed by her long-suffering mother, who accepts the outrageous behavior of her second alcoholic husband (thereby enabling him to stay drunk) because she feels this is her lot in life or, as she puts it, "It was meant to be this way." Her daughter, following in her footsteps, adopts the same fatalistic attitude. She goes through life profoundly depressed, with a sense of bleakness that pervades all she does. Her only escape is at the gambling tables.

Children of alcoholics also learn early to put aside their own needs. Any request for understanding or help has to be timed to the alcoholic's ability to listen or to react, often long after the child needs the help. Now, as adults, these children put off getting what they need. They've had a lot of practice ignoring their own distress signals.

Another, perhaps more subtle reason that adult children of alcoholics don't search for help is that they fail to recognize that anything is wrong or that an opportunity exists to improve the quality of their lives. They don't connect the troubles they are having as adults with the drinking they lived with. They may not even remember the drinking. "Some people in our group of adult children of alcoholics," says the leader, "don't recall what happened during their childhood until they've been in the group for months." In addition, they don't consciously acknowledge the pain, even if they feel it. A dulled self-consciousness can be traced back to childhood too; it is a protective mechanism that serves as a cover-up but not as a solution. Children of alcoholics were told, inferentially or directly, to blot out the realities and many did just that. Some do not remember how awful things felt and how bleak the world looked.

Some families are too proud to ask for help. They would rather do without than ask. Others believe in self-sufficiency and assume that asking for help is a sign of self-indulgence and should not be catered to. If you come from a family that traditionally does not look for help outside the family, the possibility of getting anything at all from strangers may simply never have occurred to you.

You may also put off treatment by using time-honored ways of avoiding problems. You make excuses to yourself (it's their problem, not mine) or procrastinate (no time, too busy, have enough to think about, let bygones be bygones). Or you ask, "What can it do for me anyway?" These all stop you from coming to grips with your problems.

A more realistic barrier to accepting professional help is cost. However, there are usually ways of getting the services you need without going to great expense. Some therapists charge on a sliding scale so that you pay in accordance with your income. Some will cut the fee or will work on a no-fee basis with a limited number of patients. Don't be reticent about asking about fees. Your therapist will expect the questions.

In addition to private therapists, there are clinics and tax-supported facilities where you will be expected to pay only a minimal amount. You can find most of them listed in the phone book under community health or mental health services. Many health insurance policies will cover at least part of your treatment.

If you feel poor right now, perhaps you can ask a relative to lend you the money. Also, it might be worth reconsidering your list of spending priorities. Funds spent on your own mental health are well spent; treatment could change the course of your life. In addition to or as an alternative to professional therapy, there are the unique no-cost resources of Alcoholics Anonymous, Al-Anon, and Alateen. More about them soon.

How to Choose a Therapist

A middle-aged actor described his search for a therapist this way: "The first woman I saw began to cry as I started to tell her about myself. She sat there sniveling into sheets of tissue, which I assumed had been placed on the table between us for the benefit of the patient, not the therapist. When I left I decided that even though I had been looking for sympathy, enough of hers was too much. The next person I saw was someone whose office was literally filled with dead or dying plants. I asked myself, 'This is supposed to be a nurturing atmosphere?' and out I went. Luckily, I next found the man I'm seeing now."

How can you choose a therapist who will be beneficial to you? Psychotherapy must provide you with an opportunity for learning about yourself, so a therapist should be able to give you new insights into the nature and origins of your problems and then help you find ways of grappling with them. A therapist whose knowledge of alcoholism is limited may have difficulty thoroughly understanding the dynamics of your family. Yet what counts is not so much what he or she knows as how he or she feels about people who drink too much. If a therapist holds a negative or punitive attitude toward drunkenness and drinking, your treatment may be hampered. The negative attitude will come across as disapproval or nonacceptance, and it will be hard for you to discuss what actually went on without feeling ashamed, embarrassed, or inferior.

The therapist you choose should not view alcoholism as a symptom of an underlying disturbance or a manifestation of a weak ego. An appropriate therapist must:

1. Accept alcoholism as an illness and know that the alcoholic is a sick person and that much dreadful conduct may be related to the action of alcohol on the brain. That does not mean, however, that the therapist should believe that the alcoholic should be excused no matter what or pardoned for behavior but should be offered the help and understanding that any sick person merits.

2. Be clear in the belief that the alcoholic does not create family stress purposefully or with retribution in mind.

3. Believe that where alcoholism is linked to poverty and neglect it is not the poverty that leads to alcoholism but the alcoholism that more often leads to poverty and neglect.

4. Understand the meaning of blackouts, slips, d.t.'s, and other symptoms or consequences of drinking.

5. Be familiar with AA and Al-Anon recovery programs.

It is inconsequential whether the therapist's understanding comes from clinical or personal experience or both, as long as it is there. Keep in mind that a therapist's job is to help you. It is tempting to focus on the drinker and blame the alcoholic for everything, or to view problems only in terms of alcohol. A therapist who is too sympathetic or who does not look beyond parental drinking may miss other things. Of course, the drinking behavior must be dealt with directly and frankly and not skipped over, or treatment may be ineffectual. But a therapist who sees the alcoholic as disgusting, obnoxious, sinful, or just plain pitiable cannot help you come to a full understanding of yourself in relation to the family you come from.

Before your first interview with a new therapist, you should have in mind some specific questions. Without putting the therapist on the defensive by being overtly challenging, you might ask:

1. Why is alcoholism considered an illness?

2. Are alcoholic families different from other families? If so, in what way?

3. How about Al-Anon? Maybe that's where I should be.

4. Have you treated other people with alcoholic parents?

Bring up topics such as your own drinking, your difficulty trusting, and your troubles with long-term relationships, and see what the therapist has to say.

From responses to your questions and comments you will get an idea of how familiar the therapist is with families in which there are drinking problems. You will also want to be aware of the feelings you had while you were with the therapist. Were you so ill at ease that you couldn't keep your mind on what you came for? Did you start thinking about the grocery list or the caterpillar infestation instead of the situation at hand? Did the therapist seem involved, interested, empathetic? Did he or she really listen? (A young woman wrote in a thank-you note to her therapist: "It's such a rare experience to be totally listened to.") When the interview drew to a close, did you wish it would go on? After you left, did you feel you had had a positive experience? Did you learn anything? Are you looking forward to the next session?

There are some other factors to consider: Do you want to work with a woman or a man? Does age matter? Is geographic location (convenience) an important consideration? Are the personal lifestyle and political, religious, or sexual orientation of a therapist important to you? Are academic degrees, professional memberships, and number of years of experience of concern to you? People who have had rigorous training and competent supervision themselves are more likely to be reliable and therefore most helpful. And often the best therapist is one who has had personal experience as a patient—who has, in a sense, been on the other side of the desk or on the couch.

If you've had several interviews with a therapist and don't feel good about any of them, don't think that you're obliged to confine your search to just one therapist. Some of the discomfort you feel may be a necessary or integral part of the therapy itself and should be worked out with the person you are seeing. But, at the same time, you are the consumer in this situation and you have a right to comparison-shop. One "shopper" reports: "This woman therapist was wearing a purple sweatsuit, jogging shoes, and a yellow sweatband around her head. All I could think of as we talked was that she was about to leap up and go for a run. I'm sure there are others who would not have been so preoccupied by her outfit. They might not have thought it unusual or threatening. In fact, I have a friend who told me that a therapist could be wearing feathers and it wouldn't make any difference. But for me, even if her training had been excellent, her manner attentive, and so on, her inappropriate clothing made me uncomfortable and unable to concentrate on what I had come for. This was not the therapist for me, and I knew it right away."

If you have begun therapy and find that you are not feeling better, are becoming more and more depressed or confused, and don't think you are gaining any more self-understanding, how do you disentangle from such a situation? The first step is to summon up your courage and discuss your doubts. If you have tendencies toward people-pleasing, you're going to have a more difficult time than if you can just come out and say, "I don't think you and I can work together. I'm not feeling good about what's going on." If you prefer to be a little less abrupt, you can begin by enumerating some of the good things that have happened and then go on to talk about your concerns. For example, you might say, "I think I'm getting along much better at work but I still feel resentful all the time and think that might be getting in the way of the therapy. Perhaps I even resent you." Then go on to talk about the change you have in mind. If you feel too awkward making the break face to face with your therapist, you can write a letter or make a phone call to say how you feel. But don't stick with someone who is not right for you.

On the other hand, don't arbitrarily rule someone out. An

adult child of alcoholics looking for a therapist spoke by phone with one who had been recommended to her. "I don't think I should see a man," she told him, "because I can't relax—I'm scared of men." He suggested she come in and talk anyway, and she decided after the interview that he really was the right one for her.

Some people think that the best therapist is a recovering alcoholic who has "been through it." Certainly such a person, if well trained, can be immensely effective. On the other hand, sometimes he or she may be too close to it and may still be struggling with emotional involvements and biased views. One counselor, a recovering alcoholic, admits that his need to control, stemming from his way of dealing with his own sobriety, gets in the way of his ability to treat clients. As he became aware of this problem, he went back into therapy himself.

Frequently children of alcoholics go into the helping professions. Why? Perhaps they still plan their lives in terms of their need to rescue those around them, as they did as children. Or they may be so used to taking care of things and managing people that they don't know any other way of behaving. In becoming "helpers," they can continue in the role in which they feel so much at home.

Is it really true that only people who have an intimate, first-hand experience with an illness or personal struggle can really understand how to treat it? If it were, we would have no male obstetricians, no oncologists to treat advanced cancer, and so on. In other words, no one person can experience all that he or she must treat. A psychiatrist has to deal with people who have been raped, adolescents who have pimples, people who have suffered a recent loss, depressed people, psychotic people, drug addicts, and an infinite variety of people who are in need. But does the therapist have to have experienced all these distresses in order to be helpful?

There is a good chance that you might click most easily with a counselor who is also a child of an alcoholic. However, you will have to stumble upon such a person, for it is highly unlikely that a counselor will identify professionally in terms of a parent's illness. If it's important to you, however, and you feel safe enough, you may want to take the direct approach and ask a therapist about alcoholism in his or her family.

Some say the "chemistry" between patient and therapist has to be right for improvement to occur. This is an ephemeral concept that is difficult to define, but you might have some sense of what it means when you consider how you've been attracted to friends or lovers or even to a living place or a piece of music. Choosing a therapist is more than just adding up the outward features of age, ethnic background, looks, experience, and training. The therapist may "speak your language," be tuned in and infinitely knowledgeable, and still be the wrong person. Clicking together is a two-way process: The feeling of "rightness" must come from the therapist as well as from you. If you are not in tune with each other, therapy could become just one more problem for you to deal with.

If you *are* well matched, treatment time may be shortened simply because you and the therapist feel it is going to work. Feeling compatible and understood, with the knowledge that you are receiving wise guidance, may be exactly what you need—and it may be all you need. It may take a while to find. One woman's first therapist was distant and formal. He listened to what she had to say but didn't comment or respond. "I saw him first thing in the morning," she says, "and he looked and acted like he had a hangover." (Her automatic assumption that alcohol explained his behavior is typical.) After a few months she left. Her new therapist (a Jungian, although that is only incidental) is "warm and gentle. He talks and reacts and gives me the feeling he cares. He's saved my life. He's just right for me."

Which Treatment?

Therapy has been called a "voyage of self-discovery." This discovery can be guided in many ways. There are professionally trained men and women who treat people individually or in groups, or in a combination of the two. Some treat the whole family as a group or treat several families at once. There are self-help groups that operate without a trained leader; there are the methods associated with faith and religion.

Which form of treatment is best for you depends on your needs and emotional makeup. Some people begin with one method and move to another. Adult children of alcoholics often begin with Al-Anon (or Alateen as children) and then discover later on that their problems have become pressing enough for them to look for more formal treatment.

Individual therapy is the choice for those whose natural reticence keeps them from joining groups and talking about personal problems in the presence of others. Then, after a time, they may want to join a group. Other people have trouble trusting any one individual and feel safe only among those with whom they naturally identify. In this case, of course, group therapy—often with other adult children of alcoholics—is the place for them to begin. In general, however, most people begin with individual therapy.

Individual Therapy

When two friends meet on the street and exchange light pleasantries accompanied by a recognition of caring for each other, each may walk away feeling better. The meeting was a healing one, no matter how informal. Sometimes a hand-holding or cuddle session is all you need to get through a rough period. However, you may want a more formal therapeutic relationship with a trained helper such as a minister, nurse, doctor, social worker, psychiatrist, counselor, or psychologist. The difference between a psychotherapeutic relationship and an informal supportive relationship is that the therapist has been designated as a healer by virtue of having gone through rigorous training and is then socially sanctioned to act as such. Occasionally, the two roles may overlap. You may develop a close relationship with a therapist who is accepting, encouraging, and understanding and later gain the therapist as a friend. This may prove to you that, in fact, you can form a close relationship even if you have not been able to do so before.

Studies show that it is the personality of the therapist, not his or her theoretical orientation (psychoanalytic, Jungian, Gestalt, behavioristic, humanistic—to name a few of the more than hundreds), that makes the difference. Therapeutic style is also important. A therapist may be quiet, warm, active, didactic, abrupt, authoritarian, and so on. He or she may have more or less ability to empathize, understand, support, and accept. What may be right for you may be wrong for someone else.

There are many types of individual therapy. Some are short term, aimed at dealing with a crisis. Others extend over longer periods of time, with more or less emphasis on the present rather than on the past. If you are looking for in-depth treatment, you may want to consider psychoanalysis or psychoanalytically oriented psychotherapy. It is usually more costly in terms of both time and money. And it can be more painful, since you will be actively probing into your unconscious, your past, your dreams. You will work on buried emotions that stem from earlier times but that still govern your thinking and behavior.

Several attributes of individual therapy may be particularly helpful to you as the child of an alcoholic. One is that the therapist is there for you and for you alone. You don't have to share the therapist with anyone else and you will be the subject of undivided attention. This may be a first if you have come from a household where it was difficult to get anyone to listen at all. Because you know that the time is allotted to you, you may be able to think with a clarity and an awareness that you have been unable to experience outside the therapist's room.

For some, an ordinary interruption of everyday life, such as a telephone call or a siren in the street, is so disrupting that the chain of thought is lost. More than that, a sense of anger creeps in as the individual experiences the familiar episode.

Another beneficial aspect of individual therapy is that you can usually build trust relatively quickly between yourself and your therapist. When you are reassured and made to feel understood, you soon begin to feel comfortable enough to share intimacies that previously were too difficult to talk about.

Individual therapy encourages the sharing of topics that may have been forbidden, embarrassing, or private—intimacies that were not to be shared with another human being, particularly one who is a complete stranger. As it turns out, the fact that the therapist is not related to you and has no vested interest in your family or friends is an advantage. No sides are taken and there are no power lineups or allegiances. Nor are there preconceived notions of who's right, who's wrong, who deserves what, and so on. Most of the concerns that usually hamper objective interchanges within families or between friends are not there. There are no grudges hovering behind the therapist's purpose, no ax to grind. There is only a relatively neutral person who is there primarily to help you solve the problems that you bring with you.

One more advantage of individual therapy (particularly psychoanalysis) is the special relationship that builds up between therapist and client or patient. The patient projects onto the therapist feelings and attributes that come from within and that have little or nothing to do with who the therapist actually is. This affords an opportunity to look at what is projected as a product of the client's early environment and, as such, it may help to clarify or explain the patient's unfulfilled or contradictory needs. Usually known as "transference," this phenomenon is central to psychoanalytic treatment but is present between patient and therapist in nearly every treatment situation. When it is recognized and utilized, it becomes a tool to enable the patient to remember and relive feelings that may never before have been available or comprehensible. It is in just such circumstances that some people recognize the alcoholism in one or both parents and finally come to acknowledge that something was wrong. Before this realization, such people may always have believed that the alcoholic behavior, particularly when there were two sick parents, was normal.

Because of the intensity of individual treatment, you may be moved more quickly toward making comprehensive assessments of yourself. However, group therapy also has its advantages and warrants your consideration.

Group Therapy

There is no doubt about it, people need to talk to one another about the circumstances of their lives. Groups provide a nonthreatening place to meet others with whom you have a tremendous amount in common. How beneficial a group will be for you depends on how it is run, who runs it, and how motivated people are to make changes. Like all therapies, group therapy is no cureall, but it does provide a setting for work to be done as people share feelings honestly in protected surroundings.

Most groups are limited to five to eight people. However, some are more like classes and may include up to thirty people. They usually meet once a week, most often for an hour and a half. The structure varies with the style and goals of the leader. Some groups are open-ended—members may join or leave at any time—but most are closed to newcomers and continue for a prearranged number of weeks or months. Some groups have problem-oriented sessions with the topic for the day chosen ahead of time—self-esteem or what to do about a coming holiday, for instance—or with time set aside for one group member to deal with a specific crisis.

Confidentiality is central to the integrity of all groups and it must be accepted and understood by everyone, for it is crucial to the trust-building process. It is the only way to proceed so that people will feel safe. To ensure it, members agree not to talk outside about what goes on in sessions, and often participants are known only by their first names. Well-trained leaders expedite the group's learning process by making sure that members carry out their commitments. Members need to be clear about the group's comings and goings, the format of meetings, and all "housekeeping" matters. Children of alcoholics are too used to broken promises, switched plans, and obscure reasoning.

The levels on which groups interact vary tremendously. They range from the purely didactic, in which information and education are the central concerns, to those that are psychoanalytically oriented and rely on "group process" and "transferential interactions." The latter term means that one member will project onto another his or her feelings, unconscious or otherwise—feelings from early childhood experiences that were buried and unavailable before. The group thus becomes a mirror.

A leader, along with group members, can function to help any group member affirm feelings so that the person begins to believe what he or she experiences. (What a boon for the child of an alcoholic who has spent his or her youth doubting perceptions and wondering who was crazy!) Diane, for example, announced at a meeting that she didn't know whether it was right for her to be angry at her mother's most recent outrageous behavior. This is the story: Diane's mother called to say she was crocheting a string sweater for her. Diane was delighted and immediately told her mother how wonderful it would be to have such a present. At about the same time, Cheechee, Diane's friend of many years, sent a birthday card to Diane's mother. Diane had not sent a card but had telephoned cross-country to her mother on her birthday. The next call to Diane ended with: "Your friend Cheechee is so sweet. You know, she sent me a birthday card. I think I'll give her the sweater. You won't mind, dear, will you?"

The group was outraged and leaped to Diane's defense, pointing out to her that her mother had been intolerably cruel and that, of course, Diane should be furious. In feeling her anger, Diane felt guilty, as if she were still the naughty little girl she had so often been told she was. Back then she did not dare hate her mother. She depended on her for her very life, so it made a lot of sense to bury the feelings. But now, at thirty-seven, it was time to grow up, to act more in terms of the present and to leave childhood reactions behind. The group's support helped her do this.

All members are included in the therapeutic process. A tuned-in leader senses when someone is being excluded and does not let it go by unnoticed. The leader may interpret the exclusionary behavior as a reenactment of what happened at home and may recognize the "me first, you keep out" stance that undermines the ability of the excluding one to get along with friends and colleagues. Excluding behavior is characteristic of nearly every alcoholic family. It is most often the alcoholic who is kept out, but as she or he is pushed aside or repudiated, other family members, particularly the children, learn this as a means of coping with people who may be different or unacceptable.

So there are innumerable ways a group can be a "demonstration project" on how people can be supportive as well as destructive. As they experience, learn, and work together, group members begin to make changes. But a group should not be just a place to be told how great you are, for there is real work to be done.

Groups for Children of Alcoholism

Groups for the adult children of alcoholics are relatively new, but they are springing up in private offices and mental health clinics all over as the plight of these people is recognized by professional agencies and acknowledged by the adult children themselves. The groups take various forms. Some offer supportive counseling; others are primarily educational. There is a fine line between the two and each includes some of the other. For example, in counseling, group members need to learn the basic facts about alcohol and alcoholism before they can understand their own confusion thoroughly and how they deal with it. If they don't come to the group knowing the facts, they either learn the facts from the leader or gather them from other group members. They must feel free to ask questions when they don't understand. One group member didn't realize that her parents' shakes were something other than "nerves"—that they were really withdrawal symptoms. It didn't take long for another group member to identify "nerves" as a common alibi when someone needs a drink to bring the blood alcohol level up high enough to stop the tremor.

It is common for group members to use all kinds of diversionary tactics to deny and to keep the group from dealing with discomfort. One woman who was particularly upset over the fact that her mother had had a slip and was drinking again attempted to distract everyone by bringing a puppy to the meeting. Another time, the same woman dealt with her anxiety by falling asleep. In both instances group members were able to point out how she was escaping from uncomfortable feelings.

In spite of the pitfalls, homogeneous groups are helpful. Why? A counselor from South Oaks Hospital in Amityville, New York, who began one of the first groups limited to adult children of alcoholics, says that the primary reason the groups caught on so quickly and have become so successful is because "it feels so good to be able to laugh together about the insanity. Anything that breaks the loneliness is great." Now the hospital is running a multitude of clinics—some for adult children of addicted parents (gambling, eating, and other addictive behaviors in addition to alcoholism), some for adult children of alcoholics—and is considering a group for adult *grandchildren* of alcoholics.

In a group in which all members are children of alcoholics people gain a feeling of commonality. Often members feel they have found a lot of new best friends. People usually feel more comfortable when they can give themselves a name or a label so that they can identify themselves as part of a group with commonly shared and recognized experiences. Why else clubs, alumni associations, neighborhood groups, and the like? Dr. Timmen Cermak, a California psychiatrist and president of the National Association for Children of Alcoholics, says, "Naming something gives you something to hang on to and a way to grapple with it."

If joining a group of adult children of alcoholics sounds appealing or challenging to you and there are none in your area, you might consider getting one started. If you discuss the possibility with an alcoholism counselor, a psychologist, a social worker, or a clergyman, you may uncover someone who is delighted by the idea and will help with the organizing. It might begin as a free-standing group in someone's home. Or it could be associated with a university or college curriculum. These groups are often run by university health services or come into existence as spinoffs from courses on alcohol education. Another natural place to start a group is within an already existing clinic or hospital where alcoholics are treated and personnel are bound to be knowledgeable and enthusiastic.

Self-Help Groups

A self-help group is any gathering of people who meet to give each other mutual support. There is no professional leadership, but trust and safety develop so that people can speak out and can find that they are understood; their dignity is recognized, for they all have a problem in common. Self-help groups offer a natural support system for rape victims, the bereaved, dialysis patients, Lesbians, child abusers, epileptics, and gay men, to name a few. Some groups call themselves clubs.

In *What Is Psychotherapy?* Sidney Bloch outlines succinctly the seven common properties of self-help groups. Here is a summary of what he says about them:

1. Members all share the same problem; therefore no one feels unique.

2. There is an unlimited amount of mutual support and help.

3. There is a sense of altruism among members that enables the giver to enjoy the sense of giving and serves to reduce a person's undue self-absorption and to enhance sensitivity to others.

4. The group enables members to feel a reinforced sense of normality—that they are not different or deviant.

5. There is a collective will power. Each member, simply because of the fact that he or she is there, encourages others in their determination to do whatever needs doing.

6. There is an exchange of information, some of which may not be available from books or experts.

7. There is constructive action toward shared goals.

Alcoholics Anonymous

AA is the prototype of self-help groups and serves all of the functions named above, but it is not considered traditional group therapy. It is a fellowship of men and women who are recovering alcoholics. They strive to assist each other and other alcoholics to achieve and maintain sobriety (in AA this means complete abstinence). The AA program is not a mysterious one but is based on a philosophy of twelve steps that function as a framework for recovery. The first step—"We admitted we were powerless over alcohol, that our lives had become unmanageable"—has become, over the more than fifty years since AA was founded, one of the most powerful agents for change ever devised. Its power probably comes from the fact that it represents a new beginning, a step toward "surrendering" and overcoming denial of the problem. It implies that change is possible and necessary, and it contains an inherent element of hope.

There is something close to miraculous about AA's steps and associated traditions, for they have provided a way, when accompanied by willingness, for millions to recover. The recovery is not easy for the alcoholic or for those close to him or her. Some children growing up in an alcoholic home are bewildered when a parent tries to achieve sobriety through AA. Suddenly there is a new, strange vocabulary and unexpected additions to daily life. "My father decided we had to say the Serenity Prayer used at AA meetings before every meal," a man says. "And if we brought him a problem he'd say, 'Easy does it.' He never explained why, and it just made me mad." Now you may have a better understanding of why these slogans are so important. And if you yourself have a drinking problem you may want to take a fresh look at what AA has to offer.

Al-Anon

Out of AA came another fellowship of men and women, Al-Anon, for the family and friends of alcoholics. As spouses became aware of the gains made by alcoholics in AA, they realized that they too could benefit from a self-help group modeled on AA's twelve steps. Today there are over 14,000 such groups in more than seventy countries. However, Al-Anon, like AA, is not for everyone. Some feel it relies too heavily on spirituality. Others do better in groups where they can participate more actively, and some feel the need for professional leadership, particularly when sensitive personal problems arise.

In general, Al-Anon members are female, since there are more alcoholic men than women and their wives tend to go to meetings. The result is that some adult children of alcoholics don't feel comfortable at meetings because they see so many women who remind them of their own controlling mothers, whom they may have hated. Their mothers had to take the reins in hand because of the problems of living with an erratic and undependable spouse. But, to the child, it looked as if the mother was the mean, strict one and the father was the easygoing fun lover. That view of parents often persists and makes it difficult for the adult to evaluate the situation objectively. In addition, Al-Anon places the center of attention on the spouse or individual looking for help and does not concern itself with the reintegration of the family. It suggests that "detachment" and efforts to work on your own life will afford you the best way out. For some people, a program that does not include the entire family is not helpful in the long run but just serves to split the family further. Nevertheless, for the person who takes to it, as a drowning man to a floating log, Al-Anon is a lifesaver—and if it is within reach, it should be grabbed. Chances are it will keep you afloat.

Alateen

Under the aegis of Al-Anon members, groups for children of alcoholics have found a place in the recovery network too. There young people talk about what is going on in their own lives and thus give support and hope to one another. In recent years, Alateen has been refined so that there are groups for different ages— Alatots and Postteens. Through Alateen young people learn about the disease of alcoholism, and by exchanging feelings and experiences under the sponsorship of an Al-Anon member they realize, above all, that they are not alone. Since they often meet at the same time and in the same location as AA and Al-Anon, people have mistakenly characterized Alateen as a baby-sitting service. It is not that at all.

Special Groups

Now we are witnessing a birth of Al-Anon groups specifically for adult children of alcoholics (perhaps they will be called Al-

Adults). In January 1982 there were 14 registered groups in the United States, but by December 1983 there were 194. This incredible growth is taking place because adult children are realizing, many in midlife, that the residues of childhood traumas are still with them and that, although many of their problems are similar to those of people who are married to alcoholics or friends of alcoholics, they have special needs of their own. Often the best support and understanding come from others who, like themselves, were brought up in alcoholic households. Al-Anon discussions about whether or not to open a separate checking account, what to do about car keys, what bed to sleep in when a spouse is drunk, or what to say to the boss have little or no relevance for the adult child. A format for beginner adult children of alcoholics meetings, using AA precepts, has been suggested as a basis for examining the nagging, universal question of adult children of alcoholics: "Why am I what I am?"

Most of the characteristics in the following "laundry list" are as recognizable as the spots on a measles patient. If you don't know it already, they will convince you that you really are not alone!

The problem: We seem to have several characteristics in common as a result of having been brought up in an alcoholic household.

1. We became isolated and afraid of people and authority figures.

2. We became approval seekers and lost our identity in the process.

3. We are frightened by angry people and any personal criticism.

4. We become alcoholics, marry them, or both, or find another compulsive personality such as a workaholic to fulfill our sick abandonment needs.

5. We live life from the viewpoint of victims and are attracted by that weakness in our love, friendship, and career relationships.

6. We have an overdeveloped sense of responsibility and find it easier to be concerned with others than with ourselves;

this enables us not to look too closely at our faults or our responsibility to ourselves.

7. We get guilt feelings when we stand up for ourselves instead of giving in to others.

8. We became addicted to excitement.

9. We confuse love and pity and tend to "love" people we can "pity" and "rescue."

10. We have stifled our feelings from our traumatic childhoods and have lost the ability to feel or express our feelings because it hurts so much. This includes our good feelings such as joy and happiness. Being out of touch with our feelings is one of our basic denials.

11. We judge ourselves harshly and have low self-esteem.

12. We are dependent personalities who are terrified of abandonment and will do anything to hold on to a relationship in order not to experience the painful abandonment feelings we received from living with sick people who were never there emotionally for us.

13. Alcoholism is a family disease and we became para-alcoholics (resembling and taking on the characteristics of that disease even though we did not pick up the drink).

14. Para-alcoholics are reactors rather than actors.

For an increasing number of adult children of alcoholics, these special groups have proved to be the breakthrough they have been looking for. A woman who has had five years of psychotherapy is only now confronting her anger after seeking out two or three such groups a week. Another spent the first six meetings in tears as she listened to others speak, then finally spoke up herself and felt understood as she never had before.

Family Therapy

It is easy to give lip service to the fact that alcoholism is a family illness. But what does that mean? In simple terms, it means that when one member of the family has a drinking problem, all members of the family are affected. They may all need help of some kind.

Many specialists in treating alcoholism advocate treating the whole family—but they tend to follow the AA/Al-Anon/Alateen model, with the drinker, his or her spouse, and the children all getting help through individual therapists. Other experts with different backgrounds treat the family as a unit, with all members seeing the same therapist at the same time in the same room. This method brings all members of the family together to work with one another.

The implications of family therapy are significant when the divided family comes for treatment—and alcoholic families are often fragmented. When family members are treated individually, the family remains divided. In family therapy all members get together in order to resolve their conflicts. The therapist makes interpretations and explanations and is there, with them, to act as facilitator. Sometimes family members get to know one another for the first time, for in the presence of the therapist each one finds a way to talk to the others more forthrightly than ever before.

Celia Dulfano, a family therapist and author of *Families, Alcoholism, and Recovery—Ten Stories*, says, "The interpersonal transactions of the alcoholic and spouse, parent, child, and sibling are now part of the diagnosis. They are also part of the possibilities for therapy." She thus gives credence to family treatment as a way to reach the alcoholic and effect a change by relying on the restructuring of the total family.

This restructuring is necessary because families tend to develop a homeostatic mechanism so that the "system" can survive, according to Dr. Peter Steinglass, a systems theory expert at the George Washington School of Medicine in Washington, D.C. To make this concept more graphic, think of it as a mobile—one in which, when you move one of the parts, the others all must move too in order to keep the balance. This process often shows up in families: When a sick member gets well, another family member will become ill in order to provide a continuing focus for the whole family. If it is the alcoholic who gets better, someone else may become the problem so the family can survive. This mechanism, then, tends to keep a seesaw reaction going and maintains a precarious balance. To change it, the whole family has to be involved.

A recovering alcoholic will find it particularly difficult to go back to the family where the drinking problem was spawned when the tensions and the cast of characters remain the same. How can you expect one member of the family—the outcast, the alcoholic—to stay sober or utilize freshly learned ways to deal with stress in an environment that has not changed? You can't. And this is the reason family therapy is useful, often necessary.

If you and your family have decided on family therapy and suddenly find yourselves in a room together—parents, sisters and brothers, and perhaps some others—hang on. This could be the answer. Here the alcoholic is no longer the sickest member of the family! The focus will be on all of you. What might happen? You might:

- Find out things you never knew about yourself.

- Be able to say things you never could say before.

- Find out how your fears, passions, rigidities, and so on began.

- Recognize previously unrecognized wisdom in some family members.

- Recognize the systems that work for and against your family's recovery.

In short, you might find yourself embarked on a remarkable adventure.

Multiple Family Groups

There were thirty people in the room. It looked more like a convention or a party than a therapy session. Two toddlers sat on the floor squabbling over colored blocks, three teenagers bared their teeth and compared braces, and an elderly man, almost blind, was led to a chair by his graying daughter. These were members of four families about to sit down in a circle (leaving the little ones to play) to talk about themselves, to compare notes, to help one another with anger, sadness, loneliness, resentment, and to talk about their ways of coping with persistent problems—job hunting, a degenerating hip, a broken washing machine, a girlfriend who went out with another guy, a fight between a teenager and her mother over borrowing personal clothing (underwear, at that), an adolescent's pot smoking, and so on. Each week it was different, but each week saw progress for most.

Progress means different things to different people, but generally in a group it has to do with an insight gained, a confrontation made, a resolution reaffirmed. In the safety of numbers and allies, people in this group could have interchanges with members of their own family in new and unfamiliar ways that would ordinarily bring wrath.

For example, when June complained about her father's seductive approaches toward friends she brought home, Melissa piped up immediately, "That's just what my father does. It's really gross." With contemporaries who would back her up, June felt confident enough to tell her father how much she hated the inferential sexual overtones of his behavior. Alone at home with her passive mother, whom she couldn't trust, and her helpless two-year-old sister, she had no one to stick up for her. Now she had found a safe place where she could say what she wanted to say to her father and find support from other members of the group. Many times she would risk subsequent repercussions at home just to gain the satisfaction of being understood.

Another example from the same group: A fight broke out between Marge and her husband, Ted, over a trivial matter: Whose fault was it that the car window had been left open overnight? Ted was incensed at his wife, yelled at her at the top of his lungs (the elderly blind man put his hands over his ears), and would not let her get a word in. He threatened her, saying that he could no longer put up with her negligence, would not pay the bills if she continued to be careless with their possessions, would leave if it weren't for the kids, and on and on. Several group members tried to interrupt but failed. Finally John, another group member, shouted louder than Ted, "Ted, you sound off your rocker. What's the big deal? Leave off, will ya?" Then, as John came to Marge's rescue, he realized that the way Ted was acting was familiar and was similar to what he regularly inflicted on his own wife. He looked over at her and smiled. "Is this what I do?" "Yes," she said.

Sometimes family members are so used to certain patterns of interaction that they don't hear what they say to one another. The members of another family can bring it to their attention, often enabling them to listen with more willingness and understanding than they do to a therapist. Multifamily therapy is powerful. It allows members of one family to understand their own maladaptive interactions by experiencing them as they take place in another family. It also makes it possible for one family to identify patterns in another family, calling them to their attention primarily in terms of their own experience in parallel situations. In addition, an individual who may be totally cowed or put down in the context of his or her own family may gain confidence and begin to be more assertive and self-possessed in the support group. Though this form of therapy may appear lengthy or cumbersome, everyone is learning from others all the time, even when the group is focusing on matters that might seem irrelevant to a given family.

The great difficulty with multifamily groups is the scheduling of meetings. It is inevitable that extracurricular school events, work, meetings, social activities, and unforeseen happenings will prevent everyone from getting together simultaneously. Even when meetings are scheduled at times when most people can be there, you can always count on at least one or two people being absent.

When the same people are absent repeatedly, you can suspect that their group involvement is slackening. Customarily, such matters as attendance, places to meet, and times are the responsibility of the group leader. However, the absence of an individual may make some group members particularly uneasy and, therefore, should be dealt with as it occurs. The adult child of alcoholics is sensitive to abandonment, unkept commitments, and lack of direction or leadership. Thus, ironically, a person's absence can trigger a discussion of underlying feelings which should not be overlooked or minimized.

New Therapies

During the last twenty-five years the personal search for a richer, more self-fulfilling life has given rise to a multitude of new therapies. Their emphasis is on personal growth and "self-actualization," a term used to describe the process of coming to express one's fuller, deeper potential. Many of these innovative therapies are valuable as growth techniques for "normal" people who want to expand their capacities as human beings; others use unorthodox methods to treat people with a variety of psychological disturbances; a few are comprehensive enough to deal with a whole spectrum of concerns, from dysfunction to self-actualization. As with any type of therapy, the effectiveness of a method will depend on who is doing it, how they view what they are doing, to what ends they are doing what they are doing, and the expectations and needs of the person seeking help or looking for a change.

The list of new innovative therapies is vast and includes, to name a few, sensitivity training, transactional analysis (TA), rebirthing, encounter groups, Gestalt therapy, bioenergetics, psychodrama, and scream therapy. In addition, there are self-help systems adjunctive to psychotherapy that serve to reinforce or supplement the work done in therapy. They include meditation, yoga, and body therapies (such as the Feldenkrais and Alexander techniques). Two books describe the most well known of these new methods: *The New Therapies* by Robert A. Harper, and *Handbook of Innovative Psychotherapies* by Raymond J. Corsini.

Many of the new therapies help people clarify goals, overcome resistance, reassess destructive interpersonal styles, open up a new consciousness, and improve their lives immensely. However, some of them can be dangerous, particularly ones that use more aggressive techniques or have few, if any, quality-control structures within their organizations. Therefore, you need to evaluate them carefully before you make any kind of commitment to one. The dangers are greatest for fragile people (and that can certainly include children of alcoholics) because the techniques may include probing sensitive feelings, confronting dysfunctional belief systems, and more actively seeking to uncover unconscious thoughts—techniques that can be harmful if they do not provide adequate means to process and assimilate the material that surfaces. Sometimes people in unorthodox treatment literally go to pieces. One middle-aged woman became so upset that she was carried out of a session screaming and taken to the local hospital. Barbara Schwartz, a social worker in Cambridge, Massachusetts, says, "Unless you are emotionally intact or have a solid sense of yourself, experience has shown that there can be serious repercussions from some of the new therapies. Some people cross over the border when under confrontative pressures."

With all the possible therapies—orthodox and unorthodox—choosing the right one will be a little like choosing a satisfying meal from a lengthy dinner menu. If you know something about each item before you begin, you have a better chance of making an intelligent choice.

Recommended Reading
and Other Information

Most of the books listed below can be obtained from The National Council on Alcoholism, 12 West 21st St., New York, N.Y. 10010 (212) 206-6770. A free *Catalog of Publications* is also available.

BOOKS ABOUT CHILDREN OF ALCOHOLICS

Black, Claudia. *It Will Never Happen to Me!*
MAC Printing and Publications Division, Denver, Col., 1982

> What it is like to be the child of an alcoholic and what can be done to prevent and/or cope with the resulting problems are all dealt with in this book.

Cork, R. M., *The Forgotten Children*
Alcohol and Drug Addiction Research Foundation, Toronto, Canada, 1969

> A simple, straightforward report of a study of 115 children of alcoholics written for all who are interested in children. *The* classic.

Deutsch, Charles, *Broken Bottles, Broken Dreams*
Teachers College Press, Columbia University, New York, N.Y., 1982

> A book for anyone who works with children, describing a peer-based system for intervention and treatment.

Wegscheider, Sharon, *Another Chance—Hope and Health for the Alcoholic Family*
Science and Behavior Books, Inc., Palo Alto, Cal., 1981

> Easy to read and helpful for anyone who wants to learn more about alcoholics and/or their families. It includes a detailed description of coping mechanisms and practical ways to help.

Woititz, Janet G., *Adult Children of Alcoholics*
Health Communications, Inc., Hollywood, Fla., 1983

> For and about people from alcoholic homes. Describes the characteristics of those people and gives good suggestions as to how they can cope.

Woodside, Migs, *Children of Alcoholics*
A report to Hugh L. Carey, Governor of New York State, 1982

> A fifty-page monograph with an overview of the field, a comprehensive bibliography, and excellent references.

BOOKS FOR CHILDREN OF ALCOHOLICS

Alateen—Hope for Children of Alcoholics
Al-Anon Family Group Headquarters, Inc., New York, N.Y., 1973

> An AA-based solution for children who live with alcoholism.

Black, Claudia, *My Dad Loves Me, My Dad Has a Disease*
ACT, P.O. Box 8536, Newport Beach, Cal. 92660, 1979

> A workbook for very young children of alcoholics, with simple illustrations, written by one who knows from personal experience.

Brooks, Cathleen, *The Secret Everyone Knows*
Operation Cork, 4425 Cass St., San Diego, Cal., 1981

> Forty pages of "help for you if alcohol is a problem in your home." Easy reading for teenagers.

Hornik, Edith, *You and Your Alcoholic Parent*
Associated Press, New York, N.Y., 1974

> A highly readable book on what every teenager should know, along with practical suggestions on what to do.

Seixas, Judith S., *Alcohol: What It Is, What It Does*
Greenwillow Books, New York, N.Y., 1977

> Basic facts about alcohol in a read-alone format for seven- to ten-year-olds along with clarifying illustrations.

Seixas, Judith S., *Living with a Parent Who Drinks Too Much*
Greenwillow Books, New York, N.Y., 1979

> A book for young people that offers hope, help, explanations, and practical ways to cope. Straightforward and to the point.

BOOKS OF GENERAL INTEREST

Allen, Chaney, *I'm Black and I'm Beautiful*
CompCare Publications, Minneapolis, Minn., 1978

> The personal story of a minister's daughter and her successful fight against the disease of alcoholism.

Alcoholics Anonymous (The Big Book)
AA World Services, Inc., New York, N.Y., 1955

> AA stories and history, including the twelve steps and traditions.

Dulfano, Celia, *Families, Alcoholism and Recovery—Ten Stories*
Hazelden Foundation, Center City, Minn., 1982

> An informative guide for those who counsel alcoholics and their families.

Estes, Nada J., and Heineman, M. Edith, *Alcoholism: Development, Consequences, Interventions*
C. V. Mosby and Co., St. Louis, Mo., 1982

> A comprehensive guide for nurses, counselors, physicians, social workers, and anyone interested in a single source that covers a broad spectrum of topics each written by "experts" in the subspecialities.

Ewing, John A., and Rouse, Beatrice A. (eds.), *Drinking—Alcohol in American Society*
Nelson-Hall, Chicago, Ill., 1978

> Lively, scholarly, and informatively written for the layman and others looking for a broad-spectrum book on drinking customs, drinking behaviors, and social policies throughout this country.

Finn, Peter, and O'Gorman, Patricia, *Teaching About Alcohol*
Allyn & Bacon, Inc., Newton, Mass., 1981

> A comprehensive, practical guide for teachers concerned about alcohol education. It includes a sample curriculum and instructional activities. A basic necessity for alcohol educators.

Goodwin, Donald, M.D., *Is Alcoholism Hereditary?*
Oxford University Press, New York, N.Y., 1976

A wonderfully amusing and perceptive overview of the heredity-vs.-environment issue with all its ramifications and implications.

Greenblatt, Milton, and Schuckit, Marc A. (eds.), *Alcoholism Problems in Women and Children*
Grune and Stratton, New York, N.Y., 1976 (Seminars in Psychiatry Series)

An interesting, comprehensive overview with data and theories.

Johnson, Vernon, *I'll Quit Tomorrow*
Harper & Row, New York, N.Y., rev. ed. 1980

A manual for counselors, friends, and family members describing a specific intervention technique to help the alcoholic overcome denial and accept treatment.

Mann, Marty, *New Primer on Alcoholism*
Holt, Rinehart & Winston, New York, N.Y., 1958

The classic handbook that tells what alcoholism is and how it can be treated.

Maxwell, Ruth, *The Booze Battle*
Praeger Publishers, New York, N.Y., 1976

For families, friends, and employers of alcoholics, a helpful book for anyone trying to cope.

Mendelson, Jack, M.D., & Mello, Nancy K. (eds.), *The Diagnosis and Treatment of Alcoholism*
McGraw-Hill, New York, N.Y., 1979

A wide-ranging collection of information on the medical, psychological, and social aspects of diagnosis and treatment. Detailed enough to be useful to physicians, social workers, psychologists, and alcoholism counselors.

Mishara, Brian L., and Kastenbaum, Robert, *Alcohol and Old Age*
Grune and Stratton, New York, N.Y., 1980 (Seminars in Psychiatry Series)

One of the few books on this subject, treating it comprehensively and with pertinent information and data.

Robe, Lucy Barry, *Just So It's Healthy—Drinking and Drugs Can Harm Your Unborn Baby*
CompCare Publications, Minneapolis, Minn., 1977

A guide to how dangerous it is to use drugs and/or alcohol if you are pregnant. Describes fetal alcohol syndrome in understandable detail.

Vaillant, George E., *The Natural History of Alcoholism—Causes, Patterns, and Paths to Recovery*
Harvard University Press, Cambridge, Mass., 1983

> An up-to-date, scholarly overview of alcoholism and the questions that still plague researchers in the field—with some of the answers.

Youcha, Geraldine, *A Dangerous Pleasure: Alcohol from the Woman's Perspective*
Hawthorn Books, New York, N.Y., 1978

> Thoroughly researched and thoughtfully presented material on the particular problems that women have when it comes to drinking. A useful bibliography makes this the *complete* book.

WHERE TO GET INFORMATION AND HELP

Alcoholics Anonymous—World Services
P.O. Box 459, Grand Central Station
New York, N.Y. 10017
(AA is listed in most telephone directories)

Al-Anon Family Group Headquarters, Inc.
P.O. Box 182, Madison Square Station
New York, N.Y. 10010

Children of Alcoholics Foundation, Inc.
540 Madison Avenue
New York, N.Y. 10022

Incest Survivors Anonymous (ISA)
P.O. Box 5613
Long Beach, Cal. 90800
(A recently organized group based on the twelve steps and twelve traditions of AA)

National Association for Children of Alcoholics
P.O. Box 421961
San Francisco, Cal. 94142

National Clearinghouse for Alcohol Information (NCALI)
P.O. Box 2345
Rockville, Md. 20852

National Council on Alcoholism
12 West 21st St., New York, N.Y. 10010
(Many areas have local affiliates of NCA)

National Institute of Alcohol Abuse and Alcoholism
5600 Fishers Lane
Rockville, Md. 20852

Victims of Incest Can Emerge
Grand Junction, Col. 81501
(A national network)

Index

About the Authors

Judith Seixas has a graduate degree in psychology from Columbia University, has studied at the Rutgers Summer School of Alcohol Studies, and is certified as an alcoholism counselor. She is the author of two books on alcohol for children—*Alcohol: What It Is, What It Does* and *Living with a Parent Who Drinks Too Much*. Much of the material in this book comes out of her experience as therapist, teacher, and lecturer.

Geraldine Youcha, a long-time journalist, is the author of the book *A Dangerous Pleasure: Alcohol from the Woman's Perspective*. She has written numerous articles for major magazines and newspapers on the subjects of teenage drinking and women and alcohol.